MW01049431

Leonard Lee Rue III's

WHITETAILS

Leonard Lee Rue III's
WHITETAILS

*Answers to all your questions on life cycle,
feeding patterns, antlers, scrapes and rubs,
behavior during the rut, and habitat*

Leonard Lee Rue III,
D.Sc. (Hon)

STACKPOLE
BOOKS

Published by
STACKPOLE BOOKS
Cameron and Kelker Streets
P.O. Box 1831
Harrisburg, PA 17105

Printed in the United States of America

10 9 8 7 6 5 4 3 2

First edition

All photographs are by the author unless noted otherwise.

Library of Congress Cataloging-in-Publication Data

Rue, Leonard Lee III.
    Leonard Lee Rue III's whitetails: answers to all your questions
on life cycle, feeding patterns, antlers, scrapes and rubs, behavior
during the rut, and habitat/Leonard Lee Rue III. – 1st ed.
        p.   cm.
    Includes index.
    ISBN 0-8117-1938-3
    1. White-tailed deer – Miscellanea. 2. White-tailed deer hunting –
Miscellanea. 3. Photography of animals – Miscellanea. I. Title.
QL737.U55R838   1991
599.73'57 – dc20   90-27656
                                                                        CIP

This book is lovingly dedicated to my grandchildren.
It is my hope that they will develop the interest in
and derive the pleasure from wildlife that I have.

Nicholas Leonard Rue
Rachel Christine Rue
Adam Eugene Rue
Catherine Mary Rue
Rebecca Mae Rue
Elizabeth Ann Rue
Daniel Lewis Rue

CONTENTS

INTRODUCTION

I have been observing and studying deer since 1939 and photographing them since 1945. My seminars on white-tailed deer last two and one-half hours and the audience usually asks questions for at least another hour and a half. The sales of my original book, *The Deer of North America,* and its recently expanded and updated edition are approaching 400,000, and my book *The World of the White-tailed Deer* is in its twenty-eighth printing. My column, "Rue's Views," has appeared in *Deer & Deer Hunting* magazine for the past eight years and the questions keep flooding in. All this leads me to realize that people who are really interested in deer can never get enough information; I know I can't. I have taken well over two hundred thousand photographs of whitetails, yet every time I go out I learn something new about these fascinating creatures.

On the following pages you will find a selection of the questions and answers that have appeared in "Rue's Views." My heartfelt thanks to Jack Brauer, Al Hofacker, and Dr. Rob Wegner, the owners of *Deer & Deer Hunting* magazine, for allowing me to reprint my column here. The questions addressed here could be the ones you might have wanted to ask. I hope that you will enjoy and learn from the answers and that they will stimulate you to observe deer more closely. Careful observation and an inquiring approach will increase your knowledge and enjoyment of these creatures, whether you are a hunter, photographer, or nature lover.

Thanks to you, my readers. Keep those cards and letters coming in. If you have a question on deer, send it on to me; I'll be glad to receive it.

God be with you,

Leonard Lee Rue III
138 Millbrook Road
Blairstown, NJ 07825

Part One

Deer Anatomy

I RECENTLY READ an article in the *Journal of Mammalogists* by Miller, Marchinton, Forand, and Johansen on dominance in white-tailed bucks. The gist of the article was that it is the level of the male hormone testosterone that determines dominance as much as it is age, body size, and antler size of the buck. How does this agree with your personal observations in the field?   *O. J., Albany, New York*

I have read the article with great interest and agree with it heartily. From years of personal observation in the field of all types of horned and antlered animals, but particularly of deer, I have found that the male with the largest horns or antlers is usually the dominant animal because he usually also has the age, the body size, and the hormones to go with it.

This is not always the case, however, and I can give you several examples. My good friend Joe Taylor has had a captive deer herd for years. Several years ago he had a young buck, fifteen months old, sporting a set of forked antlers as

IRENE VANDERMOLEN

Dominant white-tailed buck and subordinate buck.

his first set. Because of this buck's personal internal chemistry his antlers hardened and the velvet was peeled off about one week earlier than that of any of the mature bucks in the pen. The evident high testosterone level in this forked buck gave him a shot of "whiskey courage." With the peeling of his antlers this forked buck became extremely aggressive not only to the other bucks but also toward Joe. This young buck ran the big bucks ragged, ripping them with his antlers at every opportunity as they scattered at his approach. He was "king of the mountain" and obviously enjoyed lording it over all. A week later, when the big bucks rubbed the velvet from their antlers, stimulated by the increased levels of testosterone in their systems, the status changed at once. Whereas previously the big bucks had run from the forked buck, now they aggressively chased him. During that first night one of the big bucks caught up with the forked buck and killed him.

Recently I saw a buck with a very large set of antlers dominated by a buck that had a smaller set of antlers but that had a larger body and was evidently

The dominant buck licks the lesser buck's tarsal glands because of the scent deposited there.

older. Because of genetics the younger buck had the biggest antlers but did not have the age, weight, or testosterone level to back them up.

One thing that the researchers did not note in their findings, but which I have personally observed a number of times, is that when a doe comes into estrus her status changes, too. The surge of estrogen that stimulates her to come into estrus also causes her to become much more aggressive.

It is well known that just before a doe comes into her heat period she becomes extremely nervous, high-strung, and active. She will actively seek out the bucks and will frequent the bucks' scrapes to advertise her condition. She is as anxious to be bred as the bucks are to breed her.

I have observed that when a doe is about to come into estrus she becomes extremely aggressive against all other does that she encounters. A doe of low status instantly moves to the top of the hierarchy, but only for three to four days. When her estrus is over and her estrogen level drops, so does her status.

From left: deer hair in summer, deer hair in winter, freak woolly underhair.

C AN YOU SHED some light on the coloration of deer hair in late fall, particularly very dark hair? I have seen does and bucks with a short, black sort of mane on the back of their necks, and recently I saw a forkhorn white-tailed buck, not particularly large or old, beside the road that looked almost totally black in color. It was so dark in color (I was driving along in good daylight) that at first glance I was unsure of what it was. In forty-five years of hunting and observing whitetails I've even seen some very old, large deer that were dark gray in color, but nothing like this. *D. J., Solon Springs, Wisconsin*

A deer's summer coat is a bright russet-red coloration. The hairs are short, solid, and thin and are used primarily for insect protection rather than for warmth. There are approximately fifty-two hundred hairs to the square inch. The summer coat is acquired in June and is shed in mid-August.

The winter coat is acquired in mid-August and is retained until late May or June. The hairs are long, kinky, hollow (trapping air inside), brittle, and make excellent insulation. There are approximately twenty-six hundred hairs to the square inch. The color varies from a light brown to almost a deep charcoal gray, often referred to as "blue." Deer in open areas tend to have lighter coats than the deep, dark coats of forest deer, but this is not a hard-and-fast rule. Almost every herd of deer in almost any region will have a wide variety of shadings, even within the same peer group. A deer's coloration is a highly individualistic characteristic and is of genetic origin. As deer age, their coats tend to darken.

Occasionally a deer, as well as most other creatures, will produce an overabundance of melanin, thus turning its coat almost black. This condition is not as common as the complete absence of pigment, which produces albinos.

Although I have never seen maned deer here in my home area of New Jersey, Pennsylvania, and New York, I have seen photos and mounted deer from Indiana and Illinois that actually had short manes of hair standing upright on the back of their necks. This, too, is a genetic characteristic.

SOME DEER I **see have a large white throat patch and some have much smaller patches. Why?** *T. Y., Syracuse, New York*

The amount of white on deer's upper throats, around their eyes, and at the back of their noses is variable. It is probably genetic, determined by the amount of white that their parents had in these areas. It has nothing to do with locale or subspeciation.

WHY ARE SO **many of New Jersey's bucks small?** *T. B., McAfee, New Jersey*

New Jersey is capable of producing big deer, and it does. New Jersey has some very rich farmland and produces big deer on that land, where they are protected. The main reason that not many big deer are taken is the small size of our state and the large number of hunters.

Most of our bucks are shot the first year that they have legal antlers longer than three inches. That means that most of our bucks are shot when they are seventeen to eighteen months of age.

A white-tailed buck doesn't achieve his full body size until he is four and one-half years of age. Our deer are being shot long before they have any chance of reaching their potential growth. In the case of New Jersey the early harvest is needed because through extensive land development we are constantly reducing the size of the deer's habitat. At the same time, New Jersey is experiencing the largest deer herd that we have ever had, estimated at over 135,000 animals. Even with our very liberal hunting season—twenty-one deer per year can be taken with the different licenses—New Jersey still has more deer than we have habitat to support them.

The deer in northern Pennsylvania and Vermont are becoming smaller because of the destruction of their habitats either by overpopulation or lack of plant succession.

YOU ARE PRIVILEGED **to photograph many big deer in areas that are closed to hunters. How many trophy deer have you seen in your lifetime, and how do you judge a trophy deer?**

L. G., Flemington, New Jersey

Not many. I have been fortunate to see a lot of big deer and to photograph many good bucks, but most of them would not make the Boone and Crockett book. You have to realize that only one out of every million bucks taken each year is large enough to make the record books.

In judging the size of any animal it is imperative that you have some known measurement on which to base your judgment. I use the deer's ears. When a buck is looking at you his outstretched ears measure about seventeen inches from tip to tip. Any deer having antlers wider than its ears is a good buck. Any deer having antlers much wider than its ears is truly a trophy buck.

I HAVE HEARD **that you can tell the difference between a buck and a doe by looking at their ears? Is this true?**

E. C., Blairstown, New Jersey

Only if they have antlers between them.

This buck has a fairly large throat patch.

A nice buck with antlers several inches wider than his ears. Note the small white throat patch.

The two species of deer found in North America and two of their subspecies are whitetail, blacktail, mule deer, and key deer. Pictured here is a superb five-point blacktail.

Mule deer buck.

Magnificent eight-point whitetail.

Key deer buck in rutting season. Key deer, found only in Florida, are an endangered species.

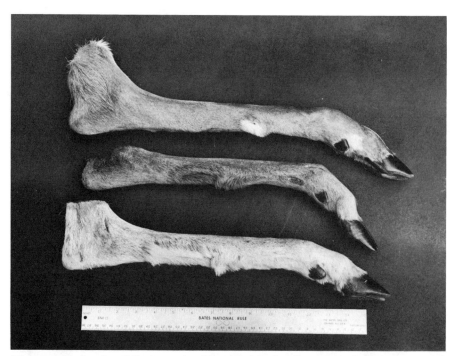

Metatarsal glands of (from top) whitetail, blacktail, and mule deer.

The tails are a good distinguishing feature. From left: whitetail, mule deer, and blacktail.

DOES WEATHER AFFECT **the size of a buck's antlers?**

M.V., Olean, New York

A definite yes. The weather at different times of the year affects the diet available to the deer. If spring and the growing season are appreciably delayed by cold weather, it will slow down the growth of the vegetation for that particular year.

A mild winter would enable the deer to seek and find more food than in a winter of deep snow, which would mean that a buck would come through the winter in better shape than normal. Of greater importance, however, is the availability of food during the actual months that the deer is growing its antlers. A prolonged cold spring delays the vegetative growth and this will prevent the antlers from reaching their growth potential.

CAN THE BASIC **shape of the antlers change from year to year?**

J. L., Fond du Lac, Wisconsin

The actual shape and conformation of a buck's antlers vary widely and are genetic characteristics. The shape of the antlers of a buck is his trademark and he will have the same type of antlers year after year. They are as individualistic as our fingerprints are, and he will pass this characteristic along to future generations. That's why different antler shapes predominate in certain areas.

The antlers may get larger in size and have more points as the animal gets older but the basic shape or conformation stays the same. A deer that has a wide-spreading rack one year will have a wide-spreading rack all of its life. Some deer have racks that are high, some have racks that sweep forward, while still others have racks with inward-pointing tips. All of these variations are genetically determined, and when a certain pattern is prominent in a certain area it is because that is the pattern of the dominant buck.

Some hunters prefer high-reaching tines while others prefer to have the antlers sweep forward majestically. Still others prefer wide-spreading racks with high tines. No one antler shape is more typical than another, and we are each entitled to prefer one shape over another. The wide-spreading racks with the high tines do score the most points under the Boone and Crockett point system.

Although the base of the antler grows larger each and every year, the size and mass of the antlers' growth each year is determined by the food that was eaten by the buck that year.

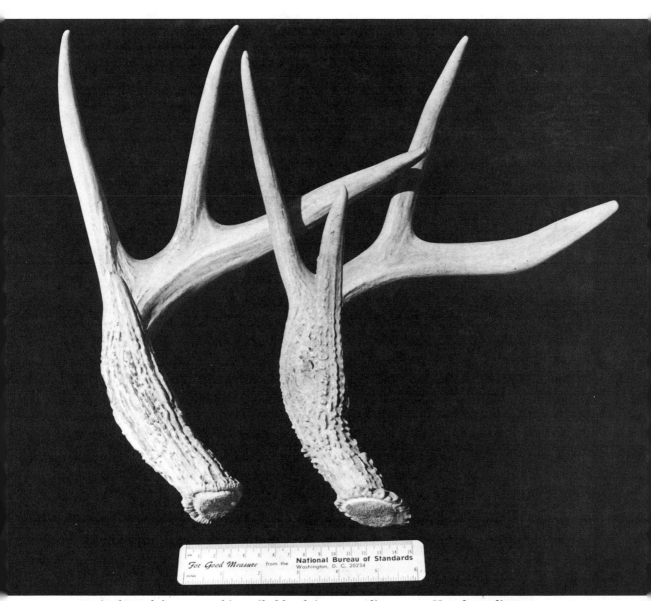

Antlers of the same white-tailed buck in succeeding years. Note burr diameter.

W HEN IT COMES to a one-and-one-half-year-old buck's antlers – an eight-pointer, a spike, or a fork – will the forked buck's antlers ever reach eight points and what will the deer's antlers most likely be at age two and one-half, three and one-half, and so forth? Will better feed at the forked buck's second year increase antler points dramatically or will his genetics hinder him?

D. H., Birhamwood, Wisconsin

Spiked antlers are usually a sign of inferior food. If a buck at ten months has been on a 16 to 18 percent protein-rich diet, he usually goes from a button buck at seven months to a six- or eight-pointer at seventeen months. Occasionally a spiked buck will be genetically inferior. As such, he may never attain a decent rack of antlers. You are what you eat, and so is a deer. Usually, given a good nutritious diet, bucks skip both the spike and the four-point stage.

Eight points is a normal rack. Although some deer get more points as they get bigger and older, most of them do not. However, if the eight-point buck continues to get good food all of his life, his rack will become much larger and more massive each year even though he does not get additional points.

W HAT CAUSES A deer to have malformed or nontypical antlers?

J. B., Peoria, Illinois

There is a basic difference between these two antler types. Malformed antlers are usually the result of some sort of injury to either the deer's body or to its antlers. Most injuries to a deer's antlers are the result of the deer running into a fence or other obstruction. Woven-wire, or hog-wire, fences cause most of the damage. Deer can easily jump over, go through, or crawl under a barbed wire fence. They can easily jump over a woven-wire fence but they cannot go through or under such fences.

A serious injury to a deer's foot or to one side of its body can cause a deformity to the antler on the opposite side of the body the following year. It is a case of the right side of the brain controlling the left side of the body and vice versa. The usual result of such injuries is that the antler on the opposite side from the injury is generally much smaller than the normal antler. If the injury is the loss of a foot, the malformation will typically result in succeeding years.

This buck's antlers were injured while growing.

Nontypical antlers are a hereditary characteristic because they occur year after year and can be passed on to the succeeding generations. The loss of a foot can cause the injured buck to grow malformed antlers year after year, but he does not pass this characteristic on to his descendents.

No one is sure just what causes nontypical antlers. Some common characteristics of nontypical antlers are exceedingly widespread antlers, extra tines, extra branching of the tines, or tines that turn downward. I personally have seen this type of mutation year after year in the same buck and have seen it in successive generations once it was established in an area.

Many hunters would rather have a nontypical buck than a typical one because the antlers of the former are usually larger. The chances of getting a trophy nontypical buck are best in areas where such deer have been taken in previous years.

A drop tine could be the result of an accident or a genetic condition.

ONE SEASON I hunted with some buddies for a week on the Upper Peninsula. Twice in the first couple of days I saw a small buck that had one antler growing down along the side of his face. I was tempted to shoot him because his antlers were so odd. I didn't because I wanted a big buck. Besides, there were few hunters in my area and I figured I might get a chance to shoot him when he got bigger. Will his antlers continue to grow one up and one down?

P. D., Grand Rapids, Michigan

That type of antler growth can only be the result of an accident. Whether or not that buck's antlers will grow in the manner you describe depends upon where the antler was broken. If the antler was broken while it was still growing and was in velvet, it will grow downward just that particular year. If the pedicel was damaged so that the top of the pedicel is pointing down, then all succeeding antlers will grow downward. I have just such a skull in my collection. The deer must have been hit by a car, and its entire frontal skull plate was broken, probably in its second year of life. The skull healed and filled in the entire broken area with new bone. Now the top of the pedicel points downward and the second antler grew down along the deer's jaw.

This one-antlered buck is a mutant.

I N THE 1988 **bow-and-gun deer season we saw and heard of bucks that had only one antler. We also jumped a buck in the gun season that had only one antler. Other hunters also saw bucks with only one antler in their area. What was the reason for this in 1988? Was it due to dry conditions or was it for some other reason?** *D. M., Sugarcreek, Ohio*

You didn't say whether the other antler was broken off or just didn't grow at all. I'm assuming the latter because you wanted to know if the drought of 1988 caused this malformation.

I do not believe that it was caused by the drought because the lack of food would have affected each antler equally. I constantly stress that the only part of a buck's antler that grows larger each year is the burr, or coronet, and perhaps the area for one inch above it. The actual mass and size of the antler will fluctuate each year depending upon the food ingested during the year the antlers were grown. A severe drought will reduce the antlers for that particular year.

If the antler did not grow at all, it is definitely a genetic condition. What that means is that, unlikely as it may seem, a one-antlered buck became dominant and passed on his genes to the one-antlered offspring you are now seeing.

Another unique set of antlers.

FOR THREE YEARS in a row I photographed a big buck in Shenandoah Valley National Forest here in Virginia. The buck had been hit with an arrow that had entered his head below and behind his right eye, severing the optic nerve. The arrow protruded three to four inches from his forehead and was broken off about one inch below where it entered the skull. The buck was blind in the right eye, which was shrunken in the socket, but the deer was healthy in all other respects. The first year I photographed him he had five points on one beam and four on the other. The second year the antlers were larger and he was a ten-pointer, having five points on each side. The third year he was only an eight-pointer.

I read in your book *The Deer of North America* that if a deer is injured on one side of the body, the injury will affect the antler growth on the opposite side of his body the following year. Doesn't the fact that this buck had three good sets of antlers, and that the one set was even larger, disprove your statement?   *D. E., Staunton, Virginia*

No, the fact that that buck had three sets of good antlers after being injured does not disprove my statement. What I said was that an injury to the lower extremities, the leg or the foot, and usually the foot, will cause the buck to grow an abnormal antler on the opposite side of the body from the injured side. This doesn't hold true if the buck is injured in the body or, as in this case, in the head.

It was most unusual that more damage was not done to the buck by the arrow. The arrow must have penetrated the rear portion of the eye socket or I doubt it would have penetrated as deep as it did. Entering the buck's head on the angle it did, it would have to penetrate the main side structure of the skull itself, not through it but horizontally along the side of the skull. An inch or so farther back and it would have penetrated the brain case and would have dropped the deer in its tracks.

You bring up another interesting point that I was asked about just recently and to which I could not give a positive answer. I was asked if I had ever seen a deer that was blind, if not in both eyes, at least in one. The fellow asking the question said he had been told that a deer could not survive if blinded in even one eye. However, try as I might, I cannot recall ever seeing a deer blind in one or both eyes. I have to agree that a deer blinded in both eyes would be most unlikely to survive. Although it would be badly handicapped, I can see no reason why a deer could not survive if it were blind in only one eye.

Your statement that the deer was blind in the one eye because the eye was shrunken in the socket answers the question for me. Because that deer survived for three years after being blinded, and having withstood a tremendous traumatic shock, it proves that deer can survive if blind in only one eye.

I would be interested to hear if any of my readers know of any deer, even a captive one, that lived after being blind in both eyes.

I HAVE LIVED in central Texas and have been a deer hunter all of my life. Some of our deer have pretty good sets of antlers, but I swear they seem to be shrinking in size all the time. Could this be the result of inbreeding?

T. M., Kerrville, Texas

In an area that has a low deer population there is a very good chance that a five-year-old dominant buck will breed with his great-great-grandmother, his great-grandmother, his grandmother, his mother, his sisters, his daughter, his granddaughter, his great-granddaughter, and possibly his great-great-granddaughter. This would definitely be inbreeding. However, it is not likely to happen in your area.

Your area of Texas, the Edwards Plateau, has the highest deer population in

Tiny spike antlers on a seven-month white-tailed buck.

the nation, with between 100 and 150 deer to the square mile. When I was down there I saw deer that were no larger than goats. The problem is not that of inbreeding but of having far more deer than you have good food to feed them. These same deer could not possibly survive a hard northern winter because so many of them would die of starvation. In your area you don't have a snow problem, nor often a severe cold problem, and some food is available all year long.

Inbreeding in your area just couldn't happen because there would be too many unrelated bucks after each estrous doe. Any single buck may have the opportunity to breed with one or maybe several of his own bloodline, but as a number of the does come into estrus about the same time, he just couldn't be in the position to breed more than one or two. For inbreeding to have a deleterious effect it would have to continue for three or four generations, a statistical improbability in your area.

Your main problem is that all of the deer are on private land and they just aren't hunted hard enough. Your herds are simply too big. The recent oil crunch is probably the best thing that could have happened to your deer herd. The shortage of easy money has forced more and more ranchers—most of them also oil men—to open their land to larger numbers of hunters. In southern Texas, where lease hunting has long been a way of life, I have seen some truly magnificent deer. I have long stated that the only way to start producing trophy deer is a drastic reduction in the total deer population, a heavy harvesting of both does and bucks to allow the vegetation to outproduce the deer herd consuming it.

I LIVE AND **hunt in the twelve-county northwest area of Wisconsin. The 1987 gun season saw a record harvest of thirty-nine thousand deer taken, with over twenty-three thousand of them being legal bucks. The winter of 1986/87 was virtually nonexistent in this part of the country. As a result, the winter kill of white-tailed deer was very low, resulting in a high proportion of yearling bucks. Although some carried spikes, many were sporting six- and even eight-point racks, both uncommon for yearling deer in our area.**

In talking with other groups of hunters in the area, ours included, it seemed that every group had shot at least one buck that had one or both of his antlers broken off. Most of them were snapped off at the base but a good many were broken off just above the brow tine.

My question is this: Is it possible that the soil could be lacking a

mineral, leaving the antlers brittle, or was there more sparring going on among the bucks due to a higher than normal buck/doe ratio?

M. S., Webster, Wisconsin

Without being on the spot to see or test anything myself, I can only say that there are mainly two reasons for the broken tines, and you hit upon them yourself.

First, there may be a calcium-phosphorus deficiency in the soil. If the calcium-phosphorus content of the soil is low, the fact that more bucks survived the winter would mean that there are more animals feeding on that soil, and, in proportion, each buck is getting less of the needed minerals.

The second reason is the more likely candidate. You stated that many bucks were sporting six- and even eight-point racks. This fact shows that the food supply was more than ample and that the minerals probably were high enough. If either the food or minerals were lacking, the bucks would not have had the nice racks as yearlings that you talk about. Since so many of the yearlings had those nice racks, it also shows that you have an expanding deer population that has not yet reached the carrying capacity of the land. The fact that you took a record number of deer in your area and that over one-third of them were does means that you should have had even bigger-racked bucks in the 1987/88 season.

Often antlers are broken off when bucks fight. When this happens, the buck with the broken antler will be the loser.

I predicted this expansion of your deer herd in your area several years ago when I conducted my white-tailed deer seminar at Telemark. All through that northwestern area of your state I saw virgin forests being heavily utilized as the aspen and birch were being harvested for chipboard, allowing a profusion of new forest growth to proliferate.

The record harvest of deer and bucks shows that the area was being heavily hunted. Quite often in a heavily hunted area the structure of a deer's society is broken up because most of the older bucks, the ones that would maintain the status quo, have been eliminated. Without the older, dominant bucks to enforce the peace there is much more fighting among the younger bucks as each strives to be the number one deer in the area. Whereas a big mature buck can discourage the fighting by visual signs, smaller, equal-sized bucks have to test one another by fighting to settle the matter.

This is what has happened in my home state of New Jersey. Eighty-five percent of our bucks are killed when they are yearlings and mature bucks are few and far between. Consequently, there is a lot of fighting among the year-lings and even the two-and-one-half-year-old bucks. I recently saw a nine-point buck that was two and one-half years old that had broken off five of his nine points, and this deer is from a limestone area where the calcium and phos-phorus are in great supply. Antlers become more brittle from the last part of November through December as they become more dry and solidified. In October and early November the spongiosa in the center of the antlers has not hardened completely and the antlers still have some degree of flexibility.

I believe your broken antlers were the result of not only having a higher than normal buck/doe ratio but also having more bucks, period. The increased fighting, not sparring, was due to a breakdown in the deer society because of the lack of mature bucks.

THIS PAST SEASON **I shot a deer that had a nice eight-point rack. What was even more unusual was that it had a third, small antler grow-ing out below the main right beam, sticking almost straight out. Do deer often have these double pedicels?**   *O. M., Madison, Wisconsin*

On page 57 of my book *The Deer of North America* I have a photograph of a deer that exactly fits the description of the deer you just shot. It has about a one-and-one-half- to two-inch antler pointing almost straight out from the base of the right main beam. Even though the main antler and the secondary antler are

Note the rudimentary third antler.

Spike white-tailed buck.

separated by a ridge of hair, both of these antlers are growing out of the same pedicel, as I am sure yours is also.

There is a piece of tissue, called the periosteum, that grows under the deer's skin, on the outside of the cranium itself, that determines where the deer's pedicels and antlers will grow. Usually they grow where they are supposed to grow, but I have seen deer that actually had three antlers growing from three different pedicels. One of these grew in the center of the deer's forehead, just above the eyes.

MY QUESTION CONCERNS **the size of bucks' antlers when I hunt. For the most part they seem to be spikes or forkhorns, with very few really good-sized racks (six points). I have hunted this area for twenty-seven years and the deer herd has always been large, with a good harvest of bucks and does taken every year. The forest is mature, I know that "farm-fed" deer usually have better racks, and I know about the genetic factor. The deer that I have taken recently were all average to good size but the racks have all been spikes. The area I hunt is in the western section of Sullivan County in New York State and the soil is reddish in color. Do soil content and composition have something to do with the smallish racks?** *A. D., Mahopac, New York*

I have not actually been afield in your area so can only go by the clues you have given me in your letter. I am sure that the reason your deer are spikes or forkhorns is because they are not getting a good, nutritious diet.

You say that the deer herd has always been large and that there has always been a good harvest of bucks and does. If the herd has always been large and the harvest has been good, you have a sustained yield. Where you have the conditions just mentioned, the deer herd probably has an annual recruitment rate of 35 to 40 percent. Under these conditions the herd is being managed to produce the maximum number of hours of sport possible by taking the bucks before they get old enough to become trophy bucks. Without seeing the statistics I am willing to bet that 70 to 80 percent of all bucks taken in your area are around eighteen months of age.

You also state that the forests are mature, which means that except for such mast crops as acorns they are producing next to nothing in the way of deer food. The preponderance of spiked bucks being taken in your area corroborates the fact that the deer are not getting enough protein in their diet. Although the deer are feeding on farm crops part of the year, there are no farm crops for them to feed on during the winter. And, if the forests are mature, there is no browse available either. Deer living under such conditions come into the springtime in very poor condition.

The color of the soil has little to do with the quality of food produced on it; however, the mineral content, or the lack of it, is exceedingly important. The soil in your area could be worn out; you may be getting down to the subsoil clays. If this is so, then even the farm crops will not be all they could be. You can't get the needed minerals out of a soil that no longer contains them. One of the greatest crimes in the United States today is the continuing loss of good topsoil. We are losing, on the average, three tons of topsoil per acre per year. When we lose our topsoil we will lose our standard of living much faster and more completely than by any other loss with the exception of good water.

HERE IN NEW JERSEY **bucks must have antlers at least three inches long to be taken legally during our buck season. I hunt an area north of Stokes State Park and many of the deer taken from that area are spiked bucks. How can I tell if those bucks are genetically inferior or if they just aren't getting enough to eat? Even though they only have spikes, most of the bucks have fat inside their bodies. If they aren't getting enough to eat to grow good antlers, how can they have fat inside the body cavity?** *T. S., Newton, New Jersey*

I know your area well because I live on the same mountain about fifteen miles south of where you hunt. On the part of New Jersey's Appalachian Mountain Ridge that extends from the Delaware Water Gap to High Point Park we have more deer than we have nutritious food to feed them. Because of the intense hunting pressure on the deer in this area most of the bucks are killed when they are eighteen months old as yearlings.

A standard method of telling if a yearling is on a substandard diet is to measure the diameter of the antlers one inch above the burr with a pair of calipers. If the main beam is between one-half and two-thirds inch, the deer did not get sufficiently nutritious food to grow a good set of antlers. If the deer is two and one-half years old and the antlers are no larger than one-half to two-thirds inch, then that is an indication that it is a genetically inferior animal.

As to the second part of your question, it is mandatory for a deer to put fat on its body in the fall at the expense of anything and everything else. It's for this reason that fawns stop all body growth in November or December. The buck deer is not mature until he is over four years of age, but he stops his body growth as well. Those does that have not completely weaned their fawns will do so to prevent the drag of lactation from interfering with the storage of fat.

The buck's antlers are determined by the condition in which he came out of the winter and by the availability of highly nutritious food in the early spring. By fall the drain of antler growth on the body is past, so in October and November what food is eaten by both does and bucks beyond their daily maintenance requirements will be converted to fat. This layering of fat on the deer's body is known as lipogenesis.

DO DEER EVER **break off their antler tines rubbing or fighting with trees or rocks? Do they ever deliberately break them off as sheep do?**
J. K., Muncie, Indiana

Let's answer the questions in reverse. Bighorn sheep, both the Rocky Mountain and desert types, deliberately break off, or "broom," their horn tips when they impair vision because of their tight, close-to-the-head curl. Dall and stone sheep do not usually broom their horn tips because most have wide-flaring

Fighting with a sapling doesn't cause any damage to a buck's antlers.

horns. Deer never deliberately break off their antlers because, except in a freak, nontypical head, the antlers never obstruct their vision.

Deer do not break off their antlers when they fight with trees because in such activity there is only pushing activity. Antlers are broken when two bucks collide with each other at high speed and with their greatest possible force. The impact force amounts to tons of pressure. That's what it takes to break off antler tips.

MY FRIENDS AND **I disagree about the horns of the white-tailed deer so we are coming to you for help. We would like to know if an eight-point buck will breed an eight-point buck. Could the offspring ever have any more than eight points? The same with four, six, ten, or more points? My friend also insists that if a twelve-point buck fathers a buck offspring, in the second year of the buck's life he will have twelve points like the father, only not as large.**

My home state of Iowa has a split shotgun season. The first season is "bucks only," which runs for four days; the second season runs for one week and contains several hundred "either sex" licenses. My friend and I both think that the racks on deer in our area seem to be getting smaller and fewer trophy bucks are being taken. I think, because of the way Iowa has had bucks only for several years, that the bucks are being shot off before they are old enough to get the big racks. My friend, however, disagrees and says that the horns are getting smaller because of inbreeding. What are your thoughts on this? *D. I., Mason City, Iowa*

First of all, let's call a spade a spade. Deer have antlers; cattle, goats, sheep, bison, and antelope have horns. In spite of that error in terminology you do know your deer biology.

The average set of antlers on whitetails is eight points — four points, or tines, on each main beam. More adult bucks will have eight points than all other configurations combined. This would not be true if more of our bucks matured. We would see more ten- and twelve-point racks if we had more bucks over four and one-half years of age. Between 60 and 80 percent of all bucks are killed when they are one and one-half years old. Yes, an eight-point buck could father a twelve-pointer. The number of points depends upon its food source, but the shape of the antlers is determined by heredity.

Deer need to fill three requirements to grow beautiful racks. The first

The three requirements for beautiful racks are genetics, age, and – most importantly – a nutritious diet.

requirement is genetic: big deer sire big deer. The second requirement is age. A buck does not mature until he is four and one-half years old. Up to this time most of the nutrition the deer consumes goes to body maintenance first, body growth second, and antler development third. After the buck matures all nutrition beyond what is needed for body maintenance can go into antler development.

The number of points is dependent on nutrition, but the shape of a deer's antlers is determined by heredity.

The third, and perhaps most important, requirement is that the deer must have a good, highly nutritious diet. That is why hunters have learned that the biggest and best deer are being taken from areas with good soils that are producing good food. It doesn't matter whether you are talking about deer or human beings, the statement "you are what you eat" holds true.

I don't say it couldn't happen, but I do say it is most unlikely for any buck, of any heritage, on any food supply, to be a twelve-pointer when he is one and one-half years old. On a diet of 16 to 18 percent protein the buck would skip the spike and the four-point stage. He might even skip the six-point stage. Bucks on a high protein diet often have six or eight points at one and one-half years of age and you are right, the dimension of the antlers would be small. The diameter of the beam grows steadily with age. However, there just aren't that many twelve-pointers around, of any age.

I also agree with you that inbreeding almost never occurs with deer in the wild. Captive deer, yes; wild deer, no.

The normal home range of a buck is one to two square miles. He expands that to ten to twelve square miles during the rutting season, which means he is covering six times more territory looking for does to breed. But so are all the other bucks. You also said that your hunting season featured bucks only. That also would remove most bucks from most areas so that the remaining bucks would do the breeding.

The antlers are getting smaller because most of the deer are being taken at one and one-half years of age. They don't really get their best antlers until after four and one-half years of age.

Iowa has good soil, and most of the deer there have access to good farm crops that have been fertilized. Your bucks should, or could, be monsters if they lived long enough, so it's not diet that is causing the smaller racks. That's caused by hunting pressure.

WHEN DO DEER **usually shed their antlers?**

J. W., Wisconsin Rapids, Wisconsin

Most deer in the northern tier of the United States will shed their antlers between the end of December and the beginning of February.

Antlers are sexual weapons. Deer do not have antlers for protection or they would keep them through the deep-snow months of February and March. The more dominant a buck is in his area, the more does he breeds, and the sooner he will shed his antlers. Bucks kept in captivity that do no breeding at all may keep their antlers through the month of February.

There are many factors, such as nutrition, climatic conditions, the number of sexual encounters, and photoperiodism, that affect a buck shedding his antlers. The earliest I have seen a wild buck in New Jersey shed his antlers was

Deer bleed very little when they shed their antlers because the blood vessels constrict quickly.

November 24, and the latest was the first week in February. Captive deer are better fed and many will retain their antlers longer than their wild counterparts, irrespective of the breeding they may or may not have done.

It does not hurt the buck when the antlers are shed. A scab soon covers the pedicel hole. Skin forms beneath the scab and it is this piece of skin that is the start of the velvet covering the new antler growth that begins in April.

THERE IS A pine thicket in which I have seen many bucks during hunting season. After the season I scouted this area many times for antlers that had been shed, but never found any. This area is not hunted much so I don't think the bucks were killed. Am I not looking hard enough or did the deer go somewhere else to shed their antlers?   *B. W., Williamston, North Carolina*

You probably have been seeing the bucks during the hunting season. I'm willing to bet that the deer go elsewhere as soon as it's over. You have four hunting seasons in North Carolina, with the buck season closing January 1. Most bucks in your area shed their antlers around the last of December and on into January. You were seeing the deer in a pine thicket, which is good protective cover, but it contains no food. As soon as the hunting pressure let up on the deer, they went elsewhere to be near food.

I know that you're doing a good job of looking for the shed antlers; you just aren't looking in the right spot.

FOR THE PAST several years I have hunted on state land in the northwest corner of your home state of New Jersey. During the shotgun season the first year I was there I harvested a young spiked buck. After I walked up and admired him I grabbed him by the spike to move him to a better location in order to field-dress him. When I did so the spike popped off in my hand. I just couldn't believe what had happened. Later the other spike got bumped lightly and it, too, came off.

After talking to the reporting agent and many natives of New Jersey I understand this is a very common occurrence, although no one can give me a reason why antlers fall off that early. I know it is unheard of in my home state of Vermont or other northern states, where we might see bucks with their headgear still attached into January and February.

When we go back to New Jersey in the last part of December to hunt with muzzle-loaders we never see a buck that still has his headgear, either on state land or private land.

Why are the deer in New Jersey ready to drop their antlers in the early part of December and why have they already dropped them by late December? Is this unique to the area of New Jersey that we hunt, or is this common throughout the state? Is this early dropping common in other states, or is it unique to New Jersey? *O. B., Stroudsburg, Pennsylvania*

The more breeding a buck accomplishes, the faster his testosterone supply decreases. This causes the antlers to shed earlier.

WHY ARE THE bucks dropping their antlers so early this year [1988]? On the first day of New Jersey's shotgun season I got a buck, and when I went to pick up his head by the antlers one pulled right off in my hand. Later in the day another one of our group got a buck and both of his antlers fell right off when the buck hit the ground. At the check station they told us of another hunter whose buck had lost one antler before he was shot. What caused this? Ordinarily the bucks here in New Jersey lose their antlers in late December or January.

W. P., Sussex, New Jersey

Antlers drop off in response to photoperiodism, yet they do seem to drop off sooner in extremely cold weather. I don't know why, or how, this affects them, but I have long said that some of our biggest bucks go through bucks-only gun season as does because their antlers have dropped off early.

The earliest I have ever seen a buck in New Jersey shed his antlers was

November 24. This occurred in 1975 in Hunterdon County, where I had a permanent photographic blind set up. The buck was the largest buck in the area and had undoubtedly done a lot of breeding. The bigger the buck, the more he breeds, and the sooner his antlers fall off.

After the peak of the breeding season a buck's testosterone level declines very rapidly. New Jersey's breeding season was three to four days earlier in 1988 than is usual due to extensive cloud cover in late summer and early fall, which was a factor in the early shedding. The testosterone level declines because of the buck's breeding activity and because the pineal gland receives less light due to shorter daylight hours. When the testosterone level drops, a layer of specialized cells, called osteoclasts, between the antler and the pedicel reabsorb the calcium of the antlers until they are held on only by spicules. These are like the tapered middle of an hourglass. Eventually there is not enough calcium left to support the antlers' weight and they simply drop off.

Despite our liberal New Jersey hunting seasons, which allow a hunter with all of the licenses and permits to harvest twenty-one deer, we still have a deer herd that is heavily skewed in favor of the does. Where the adult buck/doe ratio is one to seven or one to eight, as ours is here, the mature bucks have about all of the breeding they can handle at a given time. The bucks that do the bulk of the breeding generally shed their antlers first due to a diminishing supply of testosterone.

This early shedding is not unique to New Jersey. In fact, what applies to our state is usually applicable across the northern tier of states if our weather conditions have been basically the same.

I HAVE SHOT **a few white-tailed bucks over the years and the antlers have been different colors—off-white, light brown, dark brown, and one rack that I have seems almost brownish gray. Could these various colors be caused by the deer's diet?** *K. M., Kenosha, Wisconsin*

THIS PAST SEASON **I saw two bucks; one had ivory-colored antlers and the second buck had very dark antlers. The buck with the ivory antlers was seen in a clear cut surrounded by mixed hardwoods and softwoods. The buck with the dark antlers was seen in 100 percent softwoods. Undoubtedly he travels into hardwood terrain, also. My question is: Are light or dark antlers genetic? Will these bucks produce**

The velvet is very sensitive, so white-tailed bucks become docile and reclusive while their antlers develop.

light or dark antlers year after year, and will their offspring grow light-or dark-colored antlers? I understand that the sun bleaches antlers.

M. S., New York, New York

There is a lot of nonsense written and spoken about the coloration of a buck's antlers, and I don't claim to have all the answers. However, the hundreds of bucks that I have watched over a long period of time all started out with dark antlers that got progressively lighter as time went on.

Antlers are bone, consisting of calcium and phosphorus. They are usually darkest right after the velvet has been removed because of staining by the blood that nourished the antler growth. The antlers usually lighten steadily with exposure to sun and rain, which bleaches and leaches the color out so that when they are cast they are almost pure bone white.

I have found very little evidence of antlers being stained darker from the saplings that the deer rub, nor do I believe that such staining is more than a localized possibility. Bucks do not rub saplings with their entire antlers. Most of the shredding of the bark is done by the rough perlation on the base of the antlers, yet the antlers are generally uniformly dark all over. If the staining were the result of rubbing, the base of the antlers would be the darkest area — and it's not.

I do not believe, although I have no proof of it, that the coloration of the antlers is genetic. I believe that it is the result of the buck's environment. Animals that live in a dark environment tend to be darker in color. The dark-antlered buck that was found in the softwood, or evergreen, area would be exposed to less sunlight; therefore his antlers, as well as his body coloration, should be darker. The light-antlered buck was found in a hardwood region, where the leaves are off the trees for most of the last three months that the buck has antlers. Being exposed to more sunlight should lighten the antlers.

If you think about it, the antlers on the deer that you shot early in the season were probably browner than on the buck shot later in the season.

I N THE AUGUST **1989 issue of** *Deer & Deer Hunting* **you stated, "Usually between September 5th and 10th, the velvet dries and the buck rubs the velvet from his antlers."**

Although bucks' rubbing the velvet off is widely believed, I feel it may be false. The onset of velvet shedding is brought on by an increase in hormone levels, as you say. However, doesn't the velvet just fall off within a few hours to a day and aren't the buck rubs primarily the result of aggression? *P. L., Grand Rapids, Michigan*

In response to photoperiodism, a decline in the number of hours of daylight in a twenty-four-hour period, in this case in August, there is an enlargement of the buck's testicles and an increase in the production of the male sex hormone testosterone. This in turn causes the antlers to solidify, effectively shutting off the blood supply to them, causing the velvet to dry. As the velvet dries, it loosens from the antlers.

I compare the drying of the velvet to our having a bad case of sunburn. As

Velvet is a modified type of skin, richly supplied with blood vessels, that envelopes antlers as they grow.

new human skin is formed, it causes the dead skin to itch and to slough off, and we scratch it. On a deer the drying velvet is rubbed off, it doesn't fall off. I am sure that the drying velvet itches because the deer takes it off vigorously. I have often seen deer rub off their velvet; however, I have not had the chance to photograph it. I have photographed both moose and caribou rubbing the velvet from their antlers and they did it in a frenzy; they wanted every scrap, every hanging fringe off. It annoyed them.

The first rubbing rids the buck's antlers of the velvet. Thereafter he may make as many as a dozen rubs a day to work out his sexual aggression and frustration; to deposit scent from his forehead scent glands as an olfactory signpost; to make a visual signpost of his presence, and perhaps also of his status; and as a body-conditioning for future battles.

I N NOVEMBER 1982 **I took an eight-point buck in southern New York. The unusual part is that it was still fully in velvet and the velvet was fresh and bloody underneath. The buck's testicles had not descended down to his scrotum. He also had three antlers. What can you tell me about my "weird buck"?**   *J. P., Hamburg, New York*

I'm not sure that I can give you a complete answer. In fact, I'm not sure biologists could have given you an answer, even if you had submitted your buck for analyses. There are a number of things that could have occurred to cause such a condition.

The beginning of antler growth each year is triggered by photoperiodism. This is the reaction of the deer's endocrine system to increased amounts of daily light. As the days grow longer in the early spring, the buck's eye acts as a photoelectric cell, transmitting more light to the brain. At the base of the brain is a small endocrine gland, the pituitary. With increasing amounts of light the eyes pick up more light and the pituitary becomes more active, producing a gonadotrophic hormone that triggers the start of the antlers' growth.

After the summer solstice the days gradually shorten. Again the pituitary is affected, and now another hormone, testosterone, stimulates the testicles to enlarge threefold and the scrotum to descend away from the body. (A white-tailed buck's testicles are in the scrotum, not in the body cavity.) The dropping away from the body is done to lower the temperature of the testicles. If they were inside the body cavity, any sperm that was produced would be infertile, as sperm is easily destroyed by heat.

As the testicles enlarge, the testosterone produced also puts an end to antler growth. The antler burr grows outward, diminishing the supply of blood, causing the antler to solidify from the base toward the tip. This usually occurs in August. By September the velvet has dried; it is rubbed off the antlers sometime between the fifth and twentieth.

It is the gonadotrophic hormones that cause the antlers to grow in the first place; the testicles have nothing to do with that. If the testicles did not develop, there would be no testosterone to cause the antlers to harden. Evidently the antlers on your buck were fully developed and they may have hardened, or at least started to solidify; you didn't say. I assume that they were at least partially hardened, they just hadn't peeled.

It sounds to me as if the buck had something wrong with his pineal gland, which is a part of the pituitary system of the brain. With a malfunctioning pineal gland the buck's internal clock would be out of synchronization with the seasons.

I saw a buck at Penn State Deer Research Center that had had his pineal gland surgically removed. The buck grew antlers in the normal fashion, the antlers solidified in the normal fashion, and they peeled in the normal fashion, but they did all of these steps four months later than is normal.

The pineal condition would not have any connection with the buck's having a third antler. Again, you didn't mention if the third antler was growing out of its own separate pedicel or if it was connected to the pedicel of one of the regular main antlers. This latter condition is most common with three-antlered deer.

Large, well-conditioned, dominant bucks lose their velvet earliest. The shedding process may take only a few hours or may last several weeks.

LEN RUE, JR.

WHILE DRIVING A **back road last week, I saw a buck with antlers in velvet cross the road ahead of me and run into a barbed wire fence. The wire cut a gash in the velvet but did not appear to break the antler. The cut bled quite heavily and then stopped. Will the cut in the velvet cause the antler to be deformed?**

P. G., St. Cloud, Minnesota

If you had asked me that question last year, I probably would have had to say that I just didn't know. Now I do. Twice this spring I have seen bucks with the velvet on their antlers badly cut. In the one case the tip of the antler tine protruded through the laid-back flap of velvet. In both instances, however, the skin grew back, healed itself, and the antler growth continued undamaged. The regenerative power of the velvet was absolutely amazing.

When first cut the velvet bleeds heavily because it is richly supplied with blood vessels. But in a matter of seconds the blood vessels constrict to shut off the flow of blood. It is the constriction, not coagulation, that stops the blood flow. Humans bleed until the blood coagulates. For the deer the constriction is very important to their survival. They would lose pints of blood in the case of a serious accident to their antlers if they had to wait until it coagulated. It is the same constriction of the blood vessels that causes the antlers to bleed just a few drops of blood when they are cast, or shed.

HOW MANY TEETH **do fawns have at birth and how many teeth do adult deer have?**

W. C., Syracuse, New York

A fawn has just four teeth in the front of the lower jaw when born. The center two are known as pincers although they are more properly identified as incisors. Somewhere between the sixth and tenth day of age four more incisors and twelve premolars—three on each side of the rear jawbone, top and bottom—will erupt through the gum line.

Deer do not, nor do any of the other ruminants, ever have any teeth in the front of their mouth in the top jawbone. Occasionally two maxillary teeth, called canines, may grow in the top jaw about two inches back from the front.

Most of the time these maxillary canines do not erupt through the gums and are located by biologists who scrape the flesh off to expose the hidden teeth. The teeth can be felt even though they are not seen.

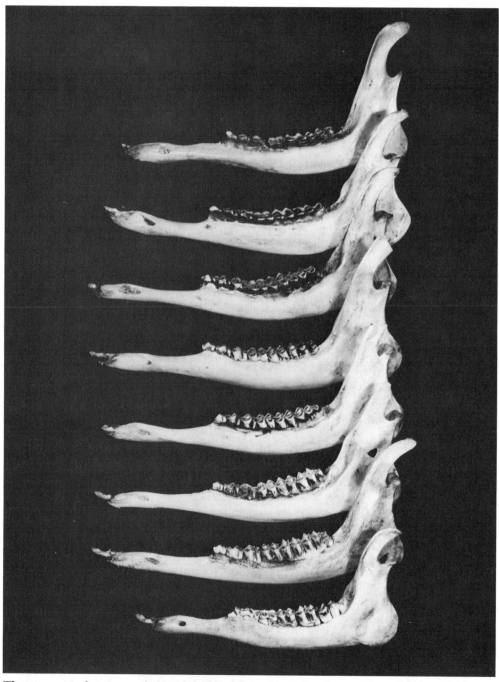

The amount of wear on the teeth helps determine a deer's age. These jawbones came from whitetails (from bottom) 1½, 2½, 3½, 4½, 6½, 7½, 9½, and 11½ years old.

Deer in the South have these hidden maxillaries more often than do deer in the North. The farther south you go the more common the occurrence. In Mexico about 40 percent of the deer have these teeth and down there they sometimes erupt through the gum and are visible. In New York State about .1 percent of the deer have such teeth; in Florida about 4.2 percent have them, while 17 to 18 percent of the deer in Texas will have them. In Venezuela between 30 and 40 percent of the deer will grow these canines. These teeth serve no useful purpose and are holdovers that have not been completely lost as the deer's teeth have evolved. These are much smaller than but similar to the canine teeth found in elk that are so avidly sought by hunters.

Of the eight incisors in the front of the deer's mouth only the center six are true incisors. The outside two teeth are pseudocanines but are similar to the incisors in shape, size, and usage, and are classified as incisors.

All of these first twenty teeth are deciduous and are referred to as milk teeth, baby teeth, or puppy teeth. They all will be shed and replaced by permanent teeth. The center incisors are shed at five months and all eight are replaced before one year. The two center pincers, when replaced, are much larger and wider than the rest of the incisors. It is these two teeth that clip off most of the browse that the deer feeds on. However, because there are no opposing teeth in the top jaw, just a tough, gristly pad, the deer cannot clip the twigs off cleanly but more or less has to tear them off leaving a stringy, fibrous cut. This makes it easy to differentiate a deer's browsing from the sharp-clipped browsing of rabbits and hares.

Fawns do not look like adult deer until their jawbones have lengthened to accommodate their molar teeth. With deer the first molar erupts through the jaw at about six months, the second molar at about nine months, and the third molar at about one year. At seventeen months the deer's premolars are ready to be shed by the permanent molars pushing up through the jawbone under them. The third premolar milk tooth has three cusps, or points, on it; however, this tooth will have only two cusps on it when it comes in as a permanent premolar. This makes exact aging of the deer at this time easy and accurate. These third premolars will also get more wear on them than any of the other teeth because they are the teeth used to cut off twigs that are too large to be clipped off by the pincer teeth.

After eighteen months of age the deer has a complete complement of thirty-two permanent teeth. Aging now will be done in the field by calculating the wear on the teeth or in the laboratory by sectioning and then counting the annual layers of cementum.

Joe Taylor with a 16½-year-old whitetail doe.

HOW LONG DO **white-tailed deer live? I recently saw a set of plaster deer jawbones showing how the teeth had worn down with age. The deer's teeth were all worn out by the time they were eleven years old. What do they eat with if their teeth are worn out and they live to be more than eleven years old?** *T. W., Detroit, Michigan*

The white-tailed deer has a life expectancy of about twelve years, although most of the deer do not live that long. In my home state of New Jersey, 85 percent of all of our bucks are killed when they are eighteen months old, when they produce their first set of antlers over three inches in length. Because not as many does are harvested as are bucks, they often live to be much older.

In the revised edition of *The Deer of North America* I tell of the oldest deer that I have personal records on although I've heard of older ones. Mine was a white-tailed doe that lived to be over twenty years old. She belonged to my friend Joe Taylor. Joe penned her up only during the hunting season; the rest of the time she ran free. However, Joe did give her additional commercial feed. As I have no deer jawbone that old in my collection, I asked Joe to save me this one when she died. When Joe tried to remove the jawbone it completely crumbled due to the lack of calcium in the bone. There is just no way that doe could have lived to be over twenty years old without being given commercial feed. And she gave birth to a single fawn at the age of twenty years.

Another friend of mine had a buck deer that lived to be twenty years ten months old. This buck, too, was fed commercial feed. A most interesting fact is that this buck produced his largest set of antlers in his fifteenth year. Deer usually produce their largest sets of antlers in their fifth through ninth years and then they begin to regress. This antler abnormality was possible only because of the commercial feed the buck was fed.

There are two outstanding longevity records from the state of Alabama. A doe that was tagged as a juvenile in 1960 was shot in 1981, making her twenty-one years old. Even more remarkable, another doe that was tagged in 1961 was shot in 1983. This doe had to be at least twenty-three years old and she could have been even older.

I recently held a deer seminar in Lynchburg, Virginia, and one fellow gave me the details of a buck killed in November 1962 in Bullpasture, Maryland, which is in Highland County. The buck had been tagged by a Civilian Conservation Corps crew in 1938 and had lived to be twenty-four years old. Most remarkable of all is the fact that the buck was nontypical and his antlers had twenty-two points. He was still in velvet when shot, although the velvet should have been peeled two months earlier. The fact that he had twenty-two points showed that he was still robust, but I believe that he was still in velvet because old age had slowed his system down. This is the oldest white-tailed deer that I have ever heard of.

It is most unusual for a longevity record to be held by a male because most females of most species live longer than the males. It is also unusual for a deer to live that long on natural food in an area where there is some cold winter weather. Deer in the South have the advantage of having warmer weather, less winter-related stress, and access to food all year round.

I HAVE HEARD that you can age a deer by the gaps between its teeth. If this is so, how big a gap is what age?   L. S., *Ely, Minnesota*

The gaps between the teeth have nothing to do with the age of a deer. It's the actual wear of the teeth and the exposure of the dentine that is used in the aging process.

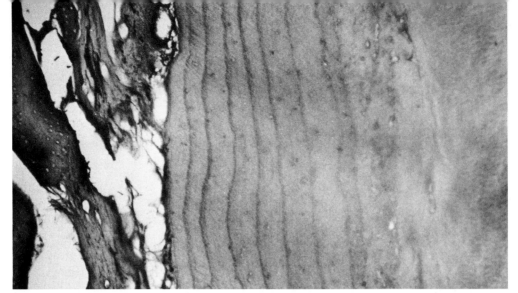

This microscopic cross section of a deer's tooth shows eight and a half years of cementum layers.

The deer's premolars and molars have sharp, sawtooth ridges on the inside of each tooth. With age these ridges wear down, the hard, light-colored enamel is worn away, and the darker, softer dentine is exposed. Since this occurs at a fairly constant rate, charts have been prepared that show the age that corresponds to the wear.

To get such a chart, at no cost, send a stamped, self-addressed envelope to the New York State Department of Conservation, 50 Wolf Road, Albany, New York 12233.

I N THE REVISED **edition of your book** *The Deer of North America* **you stated that although you used the tooth-wear method of aging deer, the extraction and slicing of an incisor tooth was the most accurate method. Just recently I heard a biologist say that slicing a deer's incisor tooth and counting the number of annuli, or layers of cementum, is not entirely accurate either. Why not?** *E. P., Birmingham, Alabama*

In my book I stated that there were many variables that made the tooth-wear method of aging quite unreliable. Actually, it is wrong in about four out of ten instances. Deer in the southern coastal regions of New Jersey will wear their teeth out faster than those in my home area of northwestern New Jersey because of the sandy grit that blows on the vegetation. The more grit, the more wear. The tooth-wear method of aging deer is, despite its drawbacks, the only method that the layman can use in the field, and it is fairly accurate. Here in New Jersey the slicing of the deer's incisor teeth is the most accurate method of aging deer that the biologists have.

Your biologist was correct when he said that the method of counting the layers of annuli, or cementum, was not very accurate, but he should have added "in the South." The layers of cementum are much more difficult to determine accurately in Alabama or other southern states because the deer do not go through the winter stress and deprivation of food that prevents the normal layering of cementum in the tooth, and that creates the visible, piled-up dark lines that are counted on the winter ring. It is the same piling-up and the production of the dark winter rings that is used to age a fish by its scales, a tree by its rings, and a bighorn sheep by its dark winter ridges. Now it has got me to wondering if the tree and fish-scale rings are less pronounced in the South than they are in the North.

IN NEW JERSEY'S **1989 doe season both my buddy and I shot our does. His doe was twenty-two pounds heavier than mine so I naturally thought that his doe would be older. When we got to the check**

Bucks continue to grow in body weight until their teeth wear down, but a doe's weight begins to diminish two or three years after she reaches maturity.

station the biologist told us that my doe was seven and one-half years old and that my friend's doe was three and one-half years old. How come my deer was not heavier than his when she was the older of the two does?   *M. C., Trenton, New Jersey*

Buck deer mature at four and one-half years of age. From that age until eight and one-half, possibly nine and one-half, years their antlers usually get larger each year if they have access to a good nutritious diet. From eight and one-half or nine and one-half years on, their antlers usually regress in size, but they continue to gain in overall body weight until their teeth are worn out at ten and one-half to eleven and one-half years.

Doe deer usually reach maturity at two and one-half years of age and continue to grow larger in body weight until four and one-half or five and one-half years of age. After this age, even though their teeth are still in good condition, they begin a gradual, annual weight decline. No one knows why this happens, but it does. This fact was proved by A. Starker Leopold on mule deer in California and by C. W. Severinghaus on whitetails in New York State.

I HAVE READ somewhere that if a doe is exceptionally fat in November during her first estrus period, she is not likely to conceive during that first period. As she will usually be a little less fat in December because of the lessened food supplies, she will probably conceive during her second estrus period. Is this true and can you shed some light on why it is so?   *J. G., Syracuse, New York*

Yes, researchers have found that obesity will cause a doe to come into estrus later than normal. Excessive fat retards development of the egg follicle, and fat in the doe's reproductive tract may prevent the fertilized egg from reaching the uterus, or from becoming implanted if it does reach it. Obesity produces a slightly higher than normal internal body heat, and that heat destroys the developing eggs. The increase in temperature would only have to be very slight. This may be why, after a particularly good autumn with a superabundance of food, many does might not breed during the first estrus period. The colder weather, the lessening of the food supply, and the lowering of the doe's metabolism before her second estrus period burns up some of the excess fat so that pregnancy then becomes possible.

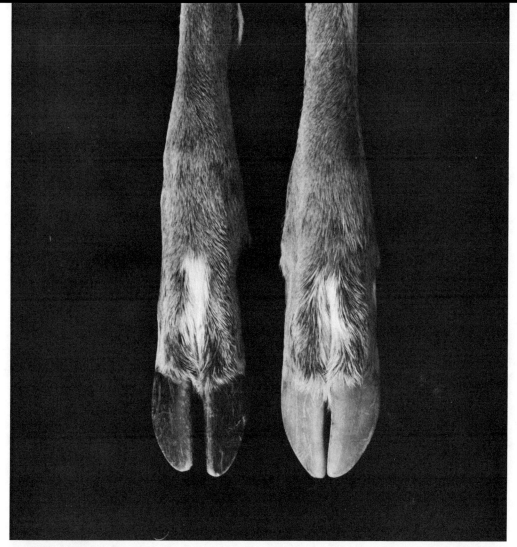

Hooves of white-tailed deer. The hoof on the left is the normal color; the one on the right is an aberration.

A RE THE DEWCLAWS **on deer actually considered toes?**

Yes. Originally most creatures had five toes; many still do. Many lost what we would consider the thumb. The deer's toes corresponding to our index finger and little finger have shrunk, becoming the dewclaws. The deer actually walks on the nails of its two center toes. The dewclaws are used only when the deer is walking on very soft ground.

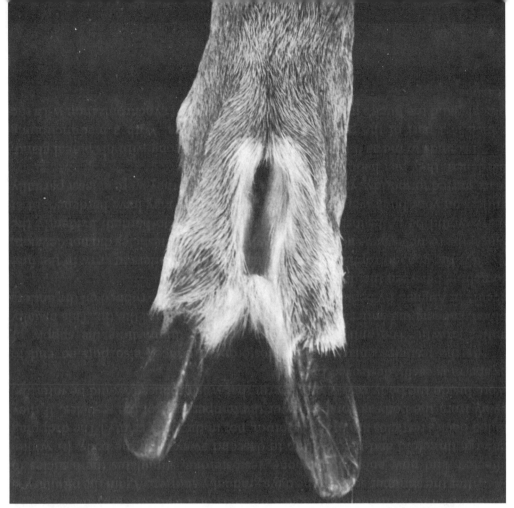

An interdigital gland is found on all four feet between the two center hooves.

A T ONE OF **your seminars you mentioned scent glands on a deer's hoof. You said that when they stomp their feet they leave a scent on the ground to warn other deer about danger. Will you give me more information on this?** *C. L., Bloomfield, New Jersey*

Deer have four interdigital glands, one on each foot, located between and slightly above the two center toes or hooves. If you run a Q-Tip up into the gland, as I have often done, you will find that the opening to the gland is about one and one-half inches deep. When you remove the Q-Tip from the gland, you will notice a rather waxy secretion that is a grayish yellow in color and smells slightly of ammonia. This secretion oozes out of the gland and down between the toes where the scent is deposited on the ground by the hooves or is brushed against grasses or leaves. When deer track one another, they do so by following this scent trail.

Some outdoor writers recommend using this scent on Q-Tips to attract deer. I say don't do it. The trails deer follow are made with an infinitesimal amount of scent. When deer stomp their feet they deposit a larger amount of scent, which serves as a warning to any deer that comes along. As long as a day later, every deer that comes to that spot will be alerted.

Anyone using a Q-Tip saturated with scent is not going to attract deer, he is going to alarm them.

HOW MANY EXTERNAL **glands are there on the white-tailed deer? A friend shot a deer with a hole through the skin over the left eye. Is that a gland or a parasite?** *C. S., Buffalo, New York*

The glands with external openings on a white-tailed deer are as follows: two preorbital glands, one in front of each eye; four interdigital glands, one between each of the deer's two main hooves on each foot; two tarsal, or hock, glands on the inside of the deer's heel on the hind foot; and possibly nasal glands, found just inside the nose.

There are also two metatarsal glands on the outside of the deer's hind foot but these are more of a cornified ridge rather than an opening. I do not know the purpose of those glands, and I have never detected a scent of any kind emanating from them.

The forehead scent glands give off scent through the hair follicle, or shaft opening. There is no external opening or gland that can be readily seen.

The hole to which you refer on your friend's deer sounds to me as if it were made by the emergence of the larva of the warble fly, *Hypoderma.* These are large, beelike flies that inject their eggs under the skin of various animals. The larvae, or grubs, of these flies develop under the skin until they are about one and one-fourth inch long and almost one-half inch in diameter. Prior to emerging, the larvae enlarge the holes in the animal's skin. When the larvae emerge on their own they leave a hole almost one-half inch in diameter that gradually closes.

I have seen caribou skins with perhaps a hundred warble larva scar marks on them. These warble larvae, in large numbers, are a tremendous drain on the host animal. Deer are also infested with warble larvae, but I have never seen more than two or three on a deer at one time. They would be a nuisance to the deer but not a life threat.

A buck rubs his forehead gland on a tree to deposit his individual scent there.

HOW LONG DO **white-tailed fawns keep their spots? I saw a spotted fawn while bow-hunting in late October.**

C. J., Appelton, Wisconsin

Most of the white-tailed fawns are born in your state between May 15 and June 15 and fawns born at that time will begin to lose their spots in late August. Actually, the spots are worn off because the spots are on brown-based hairs. The change is completed in September as the summer hair is replaced by the winter hair.

The fawn you saw still spotted in late October was born later than it should have been. Most does are bred in November or early December. Any doe that is not bred or does not conceive at that time will come into estrus again about twenty-eight days later. She can be bred only for about a thirty-hour period. If she is not bred in her second heat period, she will come into estrus a third, and sometimes a fourth, time.

The disadvantage of this is that such fawns have little chance of survival because they will not have the body growth and fat reserves to withstand the rigors of winter. It is perhaps just as well that such fawns don't survive because late-breeding genes may be passed on.

Scent deposited on tree trunks and branches proclaims the buck's presence in the area.

In warmer climates deer can breed over a long period of time, but the warm weather allows for such tolerances. The Florida key deer have been known to have young in any month of the year.

It has taken nature more than forty million years to produce the perfect animal that we know as the white-tailed deer. The deer are programmed to be bred in November/December and to give birth in May/June to take advantage of the best weather and the most abundant food. Anything that disrupts this cycle would be a disservice to the species.

W HY ARE THE **fawns of the whitetail, blacktail, and mule deer born with spots and then lose them while both the fawns and the adults of deer such as the axis, or chital, of Asia and the fallow deer of Europe keep theirs?**   *I. S., Evansville, Indiana*

It is not only the whitetail, blacktail, and mule deer fawns that have spots in this country but also the fawns of the pronghorn and the elk. The young of the moose and the bison are born with a bright russet-red coloration that darkens with age.

IRENE VANDERMOLEN

A four-day-old fawn is too unsteady to run from predators; its camouflaging spots are its best protection.

The young of the first five species have spotted coats because the camouflage pattern allows the fawns and the elk calves to remain hidden, as they all do for the first seven to ten days of their lives. Even though the pronghorn is not a forest creature, as are the other four, the young antelope are hidden by their mothers beneath clumps of sagebrush. It is the sunlight coming through the leaves of the forest trees and brush that produces the dappled pattern that allows the spotted coats of these youngsters to be so effective.

Fawns like these blacktails lose their spots when their winter hair grows in early autumn.

I don't know why the adults of the fallow or axis deer retain their spots while the adults of our deer do not; it's not because they can't run as fast as our deer do, because they can. Their adult spotted coats do make for more effective camouflage than do the coats of our deer; I just don't know the reason.

The young of the moose and the bison do not have spotted coats because in both cases their mothers are large enough and strong enough to repulse the attack of even the larger predators such as bear. Consequently, their need for camouflaged protection is not critical for survival.

IS IT TRUE **that buck fawns have markings on either side of their spines, while doe fawns do not?** *N. S., Blairstown, New Jersey*

I'm not sure just what kind of markings you are referring to. If you are talking about the rows of spots that run along the fawn's spine, then your informant is

The fawn's camouflage pattern simulates the dappled sunlight shining through the leaves of a woodland.

wrong. Fawns of both sexes have the same type of spot rows and splotches, with approximately three hundred spots total.

The sex of the fawns usually can be told by the swirls of hair on the skin covering the frontal skull plates where, in the case of the bucks, their future antler pedicels will grow. Both sexes have the swirls of hair, but the hair at that spot is much darker on a buck fawn.

THE SUBJECT IS **serious, yet I really can't recall reading too much about it: deer droppings. As an expert, what can you tell from a pile of droppings? I'd say about 95 percent of the droppings I've come across are the same — loose pellets on the ground in approximately an eight-inch diameter circle. The other type is that clump that could resemble the feces of a small horse. Would this have anything to do with their diet?**   *T. L., Longmeadow, Massachusetts*

I agree with you, the study of deer droppings is a serious business. After all, it is the most commonly found sign of deer that we encounter. Deciphering any facts that can be obtained from the droppings is very important to the hunter because it will help to give him more knowledge of the deer, its habits, and its whereabouts.

The appearance of deer dropping depends on the type of food consumed. At left are deer pellets when browsing; at right are deer pellets when eating grass.

Deer void, on the average, about twenty-four to thirty-six heaps of pellets per twenty-four-hour day in the spring, summer, and fall. They void considerably less in the months of December, January, and February in the northern two-thirds of the United States because they are on a restricted diet and their body metabolism has slowed down during those months. Fresh deer droppings are basically very dark brown to an almost jet black in coloration. Exposure to the sun and the elements bleach and leach the color from the droppings and they gradually turn to a brown and then to an almost tan color. This color change depends heavily upon the weather condition in that immediate area, but it generally takes about two weeks before the droppings turn brown. They usually disintegrate within a month. This does not happen in the winter months where the droppings may remain all winter long.

The droppings are usually one of three basic forms. They may be in the most common form of individual pellets that are three-fourths to one inch long by five-sixteenths inch in diameter. Some of the pellets have rounded, pointed, or indented ends. Although most of the pellets have smooth sides, some have indentations. I don't know why. There are usually thirty to forty pellets to one voiding. These pellets are extremely firm and are the result of the deer feeding primarily on browse and other tough, fibrous material. I believe that the largest deer void the largest pellets.

The second most commonly seen type of deer droppings are the semifirm ones that are made up of individual pellets that adhere to each other or may be compressed into a loose packet about one to one and one-half inch in diameter by two to three inches in length. Originally these pellets are, or were, almost completely spherical and are shaped by the amount of gut and bowel compression they have had applied. Many of the pellets in the center of the packet will be perfectly round in one dimension but flattened in the other so that they look like one-quarter-inch-thick Lifesaver mints. Those on the corners of the pellet may be rounded on the outside corner and triangular on the inside corner. The looseness of the pellets and their form results from the deer eating some browse but feeding mainly on succulent grasses and forbs. The larger diameter packs of pellets definitely come from the larger deer because they have larger intestines and anal openings than do smaller deer.

The third type of dropping is the loosest form and the entire waste material has no distinct form other than being in a loose mass like a miniature cow flop. This form is most commonly seen in the early spring when the deer are feeding almost exclusively on the newly sprouted grasses and in the late summer and early fall when the deer are feeding heavily on berries, fruits, and grasses with no browse in their diet.

Although I have given the times that the different droppings are usually seen, all three forms may be found at any time in the spring, summer, and fall in your particular area according to what the deer are feeding on.

Knowing what causes the droppings to take the form that they do can guide you in selecting the area to hunt based on what foods you know are available, and that can make you a more successful hunter.

DURING THE 1985 **deer season in the Upper Peninsula I saw fresh droppings the size of large marbles almost every day. Does the size of these droppings have anything to do with the size of the deer? If these large droppings were from a large buck, would he prevent the smaller bucks from rubbing and making scrapes?**

Normally our buck/doe ratio leans heavily toward the does, but this season I saw eight different bucks. The largest were a pair of five-pointers that I took. This is compared to fifteen to twenty does and fawns. I've hunted this area for twenty-five years and although those were the most bucks I've seen in a season, it was the least amount of sign: two scrapes and four rubs in the same area where other years were numerous ones.   *D. C., Kingsford, Michigan*

A survey in *Deer & Deer Hunting* magazine seems to point to the fact that the size of the droppings has nothing to do with the size of the deer. My own personal experience, however, causes me to believe that the largest deer make the largest droppings because they have the largest diameter intestines, which is where the pellets are formed. I can estimate the size of a raccoon by the size of the scat because the larger the raccoon, the larger the scat. I realize that a raccoon's scat is not pelletized like that of a deer, but I still believe there is a size correlation.

I do not know why you did not see more deer sign than usual that year because you say your buck/doe ratio was higher. Ordinarily the more bucks in relation to does will result in more scrapes and rubs because there is more competition among the bucks for the does. The bucks have to work harder and advertise their presence more as the competition increases.

Contrary to what you might have read elsewhere, big bucks do not run all of the smaller bucks out of the area. The big bucks will keep the smaller bucks away from estrous does but the smaller bucks will be hanging around the area like flies drawn to honey. While the big buck is tending the does the little bucks have the opportunity to make all the rubs and scrapes they want. It is a fact that small bucks don't make as many scrapes or rubs as big bucks do and that they start to make them later in the season.

IF DEER PUT **their heads down to browse on the ground level can they only see straight ahead? That is, do they lack peripheral vision?**

G. M., Bronx, New York

Peripheral vision is something that is usually associated only with predatory creatures, which have binocular vision. Binocular vision is caused by having eyes at the front of the head so that the field of vision from both eyes overlaps. This overlapping allows us to gauge depth of field. That is, it allows us to accurately estimate how far we are from a prey species. Peripheral vision allows us to catch the movement of some object off to the side of our general field of view. We say that we caught it out of the corner of our eye, and we did.

Deer can see 310 degrees of a circle under normal conditions because, as a prey species, they have their eyes placed on the sides of their head. They have a slight overlapping in the front of their head, giving them some binocular vision. However, most of their vision is monocular.

Most people have experienced being able to walk up on deer, providing they only moved while the deer's head was down. It is not because a deer can't see from the side, because it can; it is because a deer that is not alarmed or suspicious is concentrating its vision on its next mouthful of food.

A deer that becomes suspicious may go through the charade of eating—it may even take a mouthful of food—but its vision is concentrated on you or whatever made it suspicious in the first place. Then, even if the deer's head is down it is concentrating on you, and your slightest movement sends it bounding off. I have seen this happen many times.

WHY DO BUCKS **lip-curl?**

W. B., Buffalo, New York

The proper name for lip-curling is flehmening. All odors are molecules of chemical origin. To be smelled, molecules must be inhaled. When they are mixed with moisture they break down to their original gaseous components.

Because the molecules stick better to moist surfaces the animals that depend primarily upon scent to obtain food, to avoid danger, or to locate one another usually have moist noses. Many animals, such as deer, frequently wet their noses with their tongues to keep the surface moist to make the odors stick better.

When a deer lip-curls it is actually turning up its lip to trap the odors that it has inhaled on the very wet epithelial lining of the nostrils. The epithelium not only contains mucous membranes but also is richly endowed with sensory nerve endings. By lip-curling, the scent molecules are not exhaled with the deer's breath but are allowed to settle on the epithelium. Here the scent molecules dissolve, creating an electrical impulse that is transmitted by the olfactory bulb to the deer's brain where the source of the scent is identified.

White-tailed buck flehmening.

A buck tracks a doe in breeding season by following the faint scent of the secretion exuded from her interdigital glands.

C AN A DEER **pick up scent better left on snow or leaves (wet or dry)? And which will be detectable longer?**

D. H., Birhamwood, Wisconsin

A deer can detect scent best on damp leaves. Cold reduces all odors. A dry situation, particularly if it is warm and dry, will lift scent up and away as the molecules rise. A damp situation will hold the odor on the leaves for a long time. A wet situation, where it is pouring, will cause the scent to be diluted and dissipate as it washes away.

Of the deer's five senses scent is the most important. We humans cannot even begin to comprehend what the world of scent relays to a deer, or just how far it can detect a man's scent. Under ideal scenting conditions, which would be a day when the air is moist, the temperature between fifty and sixty degrees, and with a moderate wind blowing from a favorable direction, a deer can probably detect a man up to half a mile.

Hunters should not smoke, should not wear deodorants or aftershave lotion, or have the odor of gasoline or oil on their boots. Clean clothing and a clean body go a long way toward hunter success.

THIS PAST EASTER **weekend I was walking in the woods near my home in Hawley, Pennsylvania. I saw a number of deer, but one old doe looked like she had a bad case of the mange; most of the hair was gone from her neck but the skin did not look crusty. She was apparently otherwise in good shape physically. Her belly was swollen from the fawns she was carrying. We have had a fairly easy winter here in northeastern Pennsylvania and, although we had a couple of cold spells, we had almost no snow. Did that doe have a case of the mange?**

T. O., Hawley, Pennsylvania

I have done extensive research on deer and I have not found any reference to mange in deer. I can't say that they do not get mange, I can only say I have never seen any deer with it. I have on many occasions seen deer with gobs of hair missing from their necks and bodies, but this always occurred in the spring of the year, just prior to the deer's annual shedding of their winter coats.

Many times the dead hair seems to be an irritant to the deer and they pull it out. However, when the hair is missing from a deer's neck it has to have been removed by another deer because a deer can't reach its own neck. Deer frequently engage in mutual grooming, licking and removing ticks from each other's necks. Deer will frequently actually eat the hair that they remove from their own or another deer's body. They may be getting some beneficial trace elements from the dead hair. On very rare occasions the deer, as do other ruminants, form hair balls in their stomachs that are smooth, compact masses of hair called "bezoar" or "beazle" stones. These stones seem to result from the action of the stomach and, whereas the bulk of the hair is indigestible, the stones continue to grow slowly with time.

Occasionally deer will have a heavy infestation of lice and in their attempts to get rid of them they will eat or scratch the hair from their bodies. However, you said that the doe was in good condition so I doubt if her hair loss was caused by lice. Usually, such parasites as lice only become rampant on an emaciated deer in a weakened condition. It is thought that a healthy deer keeps

A white-tailed buck with a broken jaw.

the number of lice low by exuding a sort of repellent that comes through the skin with their hair.

I believe the deer you saw had just started her annual shedding of her winter hair early.

I HUNT IN the southern-tier counties here in New York State. One fall I shot a small six-point buck that seemed to be healthy enough on the outside, but while gutting the deer I noticed white spots on its liver. Did this deer have tularemia? I don't usually eat deer liver anyway, but I was afraid to use any of the deer's meat and I was afraid of getting the disease, which I had heard could kill a person.

D. C., Endicott, New York

If the spots on the liver were white and about the size of the head on a straight pin, there is a good chance that the deer had tularemia. However, the law of averages says it was not. The College of Veterinary Medicine at the University of Georgia claims that there have been only a couple of suspected cases of tularemia in both whitetails and mule deer. It is a very rare disease in deer, much more commonly found in cottontail rabbits and black-tailed jackrabbits. You are right in thinking that tularemia can kill people; however, the disease can be cured with antibiotics if it is properly identified in time. Since most doctors will never see a case of tularemia, they may dismiss the symptoms as being those of the flu, which they resemble. Tularemia can be spread by handling the liver or other internal organs of the infected animal if you have a cut in your skin, or you can get the disease through tick and flea bites.

If the white spots that you saw on the deer's liver were larger than pinhead size, up to the size of a quarter, the deer probably had liver flukes. The cysts caused by the wormlike flukes make the liver unappealing but they do not affect the rest of the venison. Ordinarily a deer can have a number of these flukes feeding on the liver's blood supply without any ill effects, but a heavy infestation can cause anemia. These flukes are not harmful to man, although they may be to other deer, elk, and moose.

The adult flukes in the liver lay eggs that escape via the bile ducts to the deer's intestines where they are passed out with the feces. If the feces are deposited in water, the eggs hatch and the larvae invade aquatic snails. After a period of time, and several changes, the larvae exit from the snail and fasten themselves to vegetation, which is then ingested by the deer. The larvae then migrate to the liver, completing the cycle.

WHILE RECENTLY SPENDING some time observing from my tree stand prior to bow-hunting, a number of does came by. One of the does had a large red swelling on the outside of her upper right hind leg. It was very inflamed and it looked like a red balloon about four inches in diameter. The doe did not limp nor did she even seem to notice the growth. What caused that growth, will it spoil the doe's meat, and will it eventually kill the deer?

A. P., Atlanta, Michigan

The growth that you saw was probably a cutaneous tumor or fibroma that is caused by a viral infection. The virus can be spread from one deer to another by such biting, stinging insects as flies and mosquitoes. As far as I can ascertain, there is no record of this virus ever being spread from deer to domestic livestock. It also is not transmitted to man. If the deer you shoot has such a tumor on it, you can still eat the meat as the tumor is localized in the animal's

This buck is favoring his right front leg, which is injured.

skin. Only if the tumor itself has become infected and lesions develop from a secondary infection should the carcass be discarded.

Most frequently these tumors start to grow in late April and early May. They do not seem to cause the animals any excessive discomfort. Under normal conditions the tumor just falls off the body in the fall. In the cases where the tumor doesn't drop off of its own accord, it usually is frozen off. Very little bleeding occurs when the tumor drops off, and the skin soon heals over, usually leaving a hairless scar.

I HUNT IN Westchester County, New York. Despite the high human population density, there are still quite a few woodlots that have managed to escape the developers' bulldozers. These house some mighty big bucks. They spend most of the daylight hours hiding in dense thickets of blackberry, honeysuckle, and multiflora rose, and I like to still hunt or crawl into the heart of them. Unfortunately, they are

good places to pick up *Ixodes dommini,* the deer tick. I contracted Lyme disease several years ago while deer hunting and I don't wish to get it again. Is there a tick repellent that I can put on my hunting clothes without alerting the deer to my presence? Or should I abandon the crawl/stalk method? *A. S., Katonah, New York*

I HAVE BEEN **watching for some time for more information about Lyme disease. This year there is a bumper crop of ticks in New Jersey. I would like to know if the deer actually have the disease the same as the tick. If so, is the meat safe to eat?** *G. C., Sayreville, New Jersey*

Lyme disease is spreading quite rapidly across the country, with four major regional hot spots. It occurs on the Atlantic coast from Massachusetts to North Carolina, centering on Connecticut where it was first discovered in Lyme, hence its name. Westchester County in New York had over 511 cases in 1986. It is spreading in my home state of New Jersey, although I have no statistics or numbers for the state. The second region is Minnesota, Wisconsin, Michigan's Upper Peninsula, and a portion of northern Iowa. The third region is eastern Texas and western Louisiana. The fourth region is the Pacific coastal areas of western Oregon and northern California.

Approximately twenty-five thousand people have contracted the disease nationwide. Unfortunately, most doctors have had no experience with the disease and quite frequently misdiagnose it because of the flulike symptoms of runny nose, fever, and stiff neck. The most important sign is where the tick bites a person. It usually causes an inflammation that has a red center, a light-colored ring, and an expanding red ring, making it look like a bull's-eye target. At the first indication of such a bite the person can be treated with antibiotics such as tetracycline or penicillin. Although I have read of only one death attributed to Lyme disease, patients who are not properly treated may suffer memory loss, chronic arthritis, or heart abnormalities.

Previously it was thought that the white-tailed deer was the number one host for the parasite, but on the West Coast it is being carried by the black-tailed deer. The latest findings show that some thirty-two species of birds have been found to be hosts, and this explains the rapid expansion of the disease, which now has been reported in forty states.

Neither the deer nor the tick actually has the disease. The spirochete develops in the tick's stomach and when the tick makes a meal of blood from a deer, a human, or a bird the spirochete enters the host's bloodstream. Evi-

Although white-tailed deer are carriers of the deer tick, they do not actually have Lyme disease.

dently birds and deer have an immunity to the disease since they do not have the symptoms or reactions to the germ that manifest themselves in human beings. Yes, the deer meat is safe to eat.

There is now a product called Permanone Tick Repellent on the market. It was developed in conjunction with the U.S. Department of Defense, the U.S. Department of Agriculture, and many university researchers. This product has been found to be up to 100 percent effective in repelling ticks (all life stages of the deer tick, Lone Star tick, and American dog tick), chiggers, mites, and over fifty additional biting, stinging, and bloodsucking insects. It is especially effective for use on clothing, where it chemically bonds to both natural and synthetic fibers. I spray my socks, shoe tops, and pant legs up to the knees. It is not designed to be used on the skin, but it will do no harm if done so. It's just that the body chemistry breaks down the permethrin, the active ingredient, so that it is ineffective.

A big plus for deer hunters is that Permanone, when dry, is odorless, colorless, nonstaining, and nonreactive. This product sprayed all over your clothing will allow you to crawl through the thickest brush and remain tick-free. Compared with the deet-type repellents, Permanone has been found to be more effective and without the undesirable side effects such as skin irritation, unpleasant odor, or plasticizing.

There is just one obstacle to the use of Permanone. Although it is available through our catalog, we are not allowed as yet to ship it into New York State. New Jersey residents can buy it but New York cannot. However, we expect a federal blanket permit that will open up the remaining seventeen states. The product is excellent, it is available, it is effective, and it is safe. The health of New York residents is being threatened by that state's own health department.

Permanone is available in three forms: Permanone Tick Repellent, which should be applied directly to clothing (especially pants and shirt cuffs, shoes, and socks) and not to the skin; Perma-Kill for Dogs; and Perma-Kill 4-Week Multi-Bug Killer, the latter being for control of all those bugs that get into your hunting cabins or vacation homes. One Mississippi houseboat owner says that he has the only spider-free houseboat on the river, thanks to Perma-Kill Multi-Bug Killer. It is also excellent for treating hunting and travel clothing for protection against moths, lice, and other scourges of mankind.

L AST SUMMER MY **family and I were watching four deer—two does and two fawns. Suddenly the deer snorted and dashed off. After a couple of hundred feet they stopped with their heads down and it looked like they were pawing at their noses with their front feet. What was bothering them?** *P. S., Bangor, Pennsylvania*

It sounds as if those deer were being harassed by the nose botfly. The female botfly looks like a large bee. She will lay her eggs in and around the deer's nose, sometimes even crawling up the nasal passageway. When the eggs hatch the botfly larvae crawl up the deer's nasal passage and get into the nasopharynx, a small pouch at the rear of the roof of the deer's mouth. The larvae feed on the deer's nasal mucus, gradually transforming into dozens of yellowish grubs that are over one inch long. They stay in the deer's head over the winter, crawling about, tormenting the deer beyond belief. In the early spring the worms crawl out through the nose or are snorted out. Within two months they develop into adult botflies that mate and seek out other deer in which to lay their eggs.

THE *PENNSYLVANIA GAME NEWS* **has recommended that hunters wear gloves, goggles, and face masks while dressing deer taken in areas of a high incidence of rabies. Do deer get rabies?**
D. K., Alpha, New Jersey

All warm-blooded mammals are susceptible to rabies. However, in reading all of the data that I have on it, and going through all of my research on deer, I found only one report of a white-tailed deer having rabies.

Rabies is a viral infection that affects the motor control segment of the brain, closing the system down so that it doesn't function. If rabies is treated with vaccine during the incubation period, a cure can be effected. Once a subject, wild animal or human, has the full-blown disease, death is inevitable.

Skunks, raccoons, fox, dogs, and cats are the most common carriers, although bats are carriers and transmitters of the disease, also. Cows, horses, and goats have been known to get the disease, but they don't transmit it. The rabies virus is usually injected into a victim by a bite from a host animal. The disease mixes with the host's saliva and thus enters the victim's bloodstream.

Bats usually transmit the disease by biting. Where large numbers of bats are concentrated, such as in wintering concentrations or roosting areas, victims have gotten rabies from being sprayed by the bats' urine from above. It is also believed that the disease can be acquired through the lungs by breathing air polluted by bats' urine and feces. Rabies can be acquired by either of these two methods but 98 percent of all victims contract rabies by being bitten.

Rabies is a periodic, or cyclic, disease and the southeastern section of the United States is experiencing an outbreak at the present time. Carrier animals are spreading the disease northward rapidly. The disease was rampant in Virginia, then it spread to Maryland and West Virginia and on to Pennsylvania. There have been several cases confirmed in New Jersey within the past few months and it will undoubtedly spread to New York State. A deer with rabies was reported in Hunterdon County, New Jersey, in October 1990.

At the present time there is no medical help for the disease. It can be prevented by reducing the overpopulation of deer by regulated sport hunting.

Part Two

Deer Behavior

I LIVE TO hunt white-tailed deer. I am out every chance that I have, watching and studying the deer, their habits, their movements, and their food choices. A number of things puzzle me about their food habits. A few miles from my home is a large, well-cared-for golf course with nice green grass. In dry weather the course is irrigated and each spring it's fertilized. I have read that deer prefer to feed on fertilized areas because the minerals found in fertilized plants are essential for the deer's health. The deer do feed out on the grass from time to time, but most of the time I see them feeding along the edge of the woods on all kinds of green plants. Why?

T. E., Akron, Ohio

Here in the eastern half of the United States biologists have documented almost 700 types of green food that a deer will eat. Deer are known as selective feeders because, although they can, and will, eat a very wide variety of food, they have preferences just like you and I do. Most of our preferences are based

73

on taste; the deer's preferences are often based on the protein or carbohydrate content of the foods according to the time of the year. Late winter, spring, and summer are the growth periods for the fawn fetus in the doe, for the fawn after being born, and for the development of the buck's antlers. All of this requires a lot of protein and minerals. In the fall and winter deer prefer carbohydrates because of mandatory lipogenesis, the layering of fat on the body as fuel for use during the cold winter months.

Deer are also selective in that they usually eat a varied diet because they need to balance their intake of protein or carbohydrates with roughage. Most

It is not uncommon to find large groups of deer in the winter, especially in places where there is food but no wind.

creatures in the wild will instinctively eat what is best for them.

Although deer do eat grass, they are not basically grass eaters. Their preference is for forbs, broad-leaved plants, and leafy and woody browse, because their digestive system is designed to handle such foods more efficiently and the protein content is usually much higher than it is in grasses. The fact that the grass has been fertilized makes it more attractive than usual because the deer get the bulk of the minerals they need from the vegetation they eat. They will frequent natural mineral springs or licks as well as commercial mineral blocks when they have access to them.

IATTENDED YOUR white-tailed deer seminar in Butler, Pennsylvania, which I enjoyed very much. I thought I knew a lot about deer, but I learned much more that night! One thing that really interested me was your statement that the three things needed to produce big deer were food, age, and genetics. You emphasized over and over that a highly nutritious, high-protein diet was the most important factor of all. Is food really more important than genetics?

Just recently I read a magazine article that told of game breeders buying big deer up North and taking them to Texas and other southern states to be used as stud bucks. The article claimed that if this was a one-shot deal, it was a wasted effort as the big bucks' genes would be lost in a few generations. What are your comments on this?

C. W., New Castle, Pennsylvania

I cannot emphasize too strongly that you are what you eat. In my program I always list the three requirements for big bucks in the same order: high-protein food, age, genetics.

Diet can have even more effect than genetics on the size of a deer.

Yes, food is the most important leg of this triangle. Without highly nutritious food the other two legs of this triangle will just not materialize. The best buck in the world, having superior genes, will not produce offspring having superior antlers if his offspring are raised on mineral-deficient soils and get an inadequate supply of protein.

Given highly nutritious food that has 16 to 18 percent protein grown on good mineral-rich soils, coupled with the age needed to develop properly, almost any buck with ordinary genes has a chance of becoming a trophy deer.

Genetics come into play only if the conditions for food and age are met, and it must be done on a continuous basis. If you take a big northern trophy buck to Texas to be used as a breeder, you can upgrade the local deer if they are fed a good diet, are allowed to live out their potential life span, and are in captivity. If a trophy buck were turned loose to breed with the local deer, without additional reinforcements of other trophy deer genes the genes of the original trophy deer in four to five generations would be subverted by the genes of the local bucks. Basically, it is better deer management to improve the local habitat by fertilization and by allowing the bucks to live longer before being harvested than it is to try to find "the silver bullet" by importing a trophy buck from another region.

I UNDERSTAND THAT **the best foods to plant to help deer make it through the winter are corn and soybeans. Of these two which is better, and why? Is it true that deer have to reach a certain weight or physical condition in the spring before their antlers start to develop?**

K. B., Benton, Pennsylvania

Soybeans have a very high percentage of protein; corn is lower in protein but is very high in carbohydrates. Protein is needed for growth and muscle maintenance, but the deer's growth stops in late November and they don't move any more than they have to in the winter. Carbohydrates are needed for energy and heat production. In the fall, given a choice, the deer will eat corn or acorns instead of soybeans because they are responding to lipogenesis. It is mandatory that the deer store fat on their bodies in order to survive the winter.

Soybeans would be best during the deer's growing season; they love the sprouts. The soybean is one of the highest forms of protein available to animals and man, averaging 25 percent or better. However, I have not seen evidence of heavy deer utilization after the beans have dried and the pods hang matured on the brown plant stalks.

Corn, which is high in carbohydrates, helps deer build up reserves of fat to get them through the winter.

LEN RUE, JR.

Deer will eat corn at all stages. They eat the sprouting corn, they nip off the terminal tip as the stalk is growing, and they will eat the corn when the kernels are in the milk or when they have dried. If the corn is allowed to stand for the deer for winter food, the strong stalks will hold the corn ears above the snow so that the ears are accessible for food.

If I could plant only one or the other, I'd plant the corn. The soybeans would be eaten at a time when other high-protein foods would be available. The corn would be available after the acorns had been eaten and at a time when practically no other food would be available.

No, bucks do not have to reach a certain body weight before their antlers start to grow. Antler growth begins in response to photoperiodism, the number of hours of daylight in a twenty-four-hour period. In early April the longer daylight hours triggers the deer's pituitary gland to cause gonadotrophic hormones to be released in the body. These minute chemical messengers cause the antlers to start growing. They will start to grow whether the deer is in good shape or not. However, if the buck is in poor condition, his antlers will be small. The actual size of a buck's antlers in any particular year is determined by the condition of his body up until the time of the start of antler growth and of the amount of nutritious food ingested after antler growth has started.

I HUNT IN **southeastern Pennsylvania near the Maryland border. Because of the extra rain in the fall of 1988 one of the farmers in the area did not get to harvest all of his corn from one field that is usually quite wet even under normal conditions. Then, the extreme cold and early snow of December 1989 kept him out of the field also. The deer loved it! We don't have a large deer herd in this particular area, but I have often seen ten to twelve deer feeding in this corn field. There is still a lot of corn standing in that field but the deer are not concentrating on it as they did before. Now I see the deer feeding on whatever green stuff has just sprouted. Why would they leave a perfectly good source of food after feeding on it all winter to feed on something else?**

J. C., Lancaster, Pennsylvania

Deer like to vary their diets as much as possible, and they also seek out the foods that will give them what they need at the various seasons. In the fall the deer glut themselves on acorns whenever it is possible because the acorns are exceedingly high in carbohydrates. The deer need those starchy foods because they produce fat very quickly. Also, as many of the green plants mature or

Unharvested field corn is a popular deer food in cold weather.

become dormant their food values plummet. They also become less palatable.

Corn is also high in carbohydrates. I have found that deer prefer starchy foods over protein foods as the temperature drops because they produce more body heat. Conversely, in the spring time the new green shoots are succulent and have the high protein content that the deer need for renewed body growth and replacement as their metabolism speeds up. I have found that corn is practically avoided as the weather warms up because the deer do not want, or need, increased body heat potential.

HAVE YOU EVER **seen deer eat mushrooms? If so, do they eat them on a regular basis and in large quantities?**

C. H., Jackson, New Jersey

Yes, I have often seen deer eat mushrooms. They are a favored food and deer will actively seek them out, searching along with their heads down, evidently locating them by scent.

Quite a few animals eat mushrooms. I have seen deer, elk, moose, beaver, horses, woodchucks, and squirrels eat them. With the exception of the red squirrel these animals all recognize and avoid the poisonous specimens. The red squirrel will pick the deadly amanita, but it does not eat them fresh. The squirrel takes the mushroom and hangs it up in a tree where the sun and rain leach the poison out of it. Then at a later date the squirrel will come by and eat the dried mushroom.

I do not know how deer recognize and avoid the poisonous species of mushrooms.

I LIVE IN **Virginia's Shenandoah Valley. This area is famous for its fantastic apple crop. The apples have to be washed before they are used by people, but the deer eat them when they fall off the tree. My question is this: What effect do all the pesticides that are sprayed on apples have on the deer? Do those pesticides affect the deer and in turn affect me?** *W. A., Winchester, Virginia*

I have read that we are now producing over 600,000 chemical compounds in the United States. Just how many of those compounds are toxic, or will be found to be toxic over the long run, is anyone's guess.

Truthfully, I don't know if the pesticides sprayed on the apples are harmful to the deer or not. I can't imagine anything that is toxic to one form of life being beneficial to any other form of life.

Many toxins gradually build up in a creature's body. Many times the chemicals ingested by an animal don't harm it, but the concentrated chemicals do affect the predator that is higher up in the food pyramid. A good example is the many kinds of fish found in the Great Lakes and their tributaries. These fish have such a high toxicity in their bodies that they can be eaten by humans only occasionally, if at all. Remember, you and I are the predators that are higher on the deer's food pyramid. I really don't know what we ingest when we eat deer that have repeatedly fed on pesticide-sprayed fruit. I can't imagine that it does us any good.

WE HAVE TRIED **feeding hay to the deer that come into our old orchard after the apples are gone because we enjoy watching them. They pick at the hay and will lie on it, but they don't eat it. What hay can we feed?** *L. B., Binghamton, New York*

Although I am against the idea of large-scale feeding of deer, I too feed some deer to bring them close to the house so I can watch them and photograph them. I feed whole corn because I live on the edge of a farming district and the deer are used to eating it. Also, I give whole corn because the kernels don't get wet and mold, as would shelled corn.

Deer, even hungry deer, are real snobs when it comes to hay. They will eat only the finest first or second cutting of alfalfa. I find the second cutting to be better. They eat only the leaves, not the coarse stalks. Coarse first-cutting and third-cutting alfalfa is rejected. Deer will pick the weeds out of timothy but do not want the timothy itself. They also will eat clover.

I LIVE IN **the southern part of Quebec, bordering the northern part of Vermont. We usually have a lot of snow on the ground, but the deer seem to be able to travel to feed without too much difficulty. I would like to know if you recommend feeding deer or will the deer come to depend on being fed and concentrate in that area, thus becoming vulnerable to predators. Would alfalfa be harmful to deer? What kind of food would you recommend?** *G. C., Beebe, Quebec, Canada*

Except in emergencies, or under special conditions, I do not recommend feeding deer. If in times of great hardship or starvation you want to be sure that enough deer survive to repopulate the area, by all means go ahead and feed. If the deer population is high and there are food shortages, I recommend reducing the size of the deer herd to give the natural vegetation a chance to grow back.

Feeding deer will concentrate them, which means they are more susceptible to predation. Not only are the deer concentrated, but the predators soon learn that they can be counted on to be there. It also makes them more susceptible to disease as happens when any type of animal is concentrated.

It would be best if you could cut browse for the deer. In the area to which you refer there should be some good stands of maple, which is a very nutritious deer food. If the trees are not being tapped for their syrup and if they are not of a size to be harvested for timber, cut some for firewood. Do this only in the winter when the deer will feed heavily on the set buds and twig tips. Cut the tree off about three feet above the ground and it will produce a lot more deer food the following year in the form of many sprouts per stump. Opening up a mature stand of maple will begin an entire cycle of plant regeneration, and that will produce a lot of natural deer food. If you can't cut browse, then you will have to settle for hay and commercial feeds.

Alfalfa hay is excellent deer food. They will eat the leaves but usually not

Red maple is very nutritious. In an emergency, browse from maple trees can be cut for the deer.

Clockwise from top left: red, white, and chestnut oak acorns. All are extremely high in starch.

the stems. Alfalfa pellets are also superb. Clover hay is an even better food because the deer will eat more of it; it is usually higher in protein than alfalfa. Commercial dairy rations also make good deer food and you can buy them in various concentrations of protein. If the deer are used to feeding on your field corn, then field corn on the cob makes an excellent food since corn is high in heat-producing carbohydrates.

I N 1985 WE had a fantastic acorn crop in our area. I have bow-hunted for deer for the last twelve years, but in 1985 I found the deer to be much more skittish than I had ever seen them. They just wouldn't stay in one spot, even while eating the acorns, and the slightest sound

sent them racing off in all directions. Although I was using a tree stand, it was the hardest hunting I have ever done. Is it possible that eating so many acorns affected the deer's behavior? *T. O., Wheeling, West Virginia*

We had the same fantastic acorn crop in my home state of New Jersey that year. Acorns of all kinds were everywhere. In some areas there had to be 400 to 500 pounds to the acre.

You did not mention what kind of oak trees you had in your area, and that could make a difference. I do know that you have a great many white oaks in some parts of West Virginia; however, you may have pin, red, black, scrub, and rock, or chestnut, oaks. With the white oak being the preferred mast crop, the deer eat the acorns in the order that I have just listed because that is the order in which the acorns are rated according to their tannic acid content. The white oak is the sweetest acorn, having the least tannic acid, while the rock oak not only has the largest acorn in actual size but also the highest tannin content.

I personally have not noticed that deer have become more skittish when feeding on acorns. However, I have seen them move almost constantly while feeding. Deer are not systematic feeders. When the ground is littered with fallen acorns or windblown apples they do not stand in one spot and clean up everything in that particular spot before moving on. Instead, they greedily feed on what is right in front of them and then take a few steps to feed again, stepping over the exact kind of acorns or apples that they had been feeding on. They do not "vacuum" an area, they just pick at it here and there. I have noticed that when there is a heavy fall of food they seem to feed more eagerly, almost as if they were afraid that their luck at finding such a bonanza might run out. The reason for their constant moving is threefold. It prevents overgrazing when the deer are feeding on vegetation and helps to assure a balanced diet, since they are consuming different types of food. It also makes it more difficult for a predator to stalk a deer because deer feed mainly while moving into the wind. Therefore, a predator that is stalking the deer upwind also has to move more to keep up, or to catch up, with the deer. And the more a predator moves, the more likely it is to be discovered.

Deer may actually move more while feeding on acorns because the tannic acid, like caffeine, is a stimulant. The deer may be experiencing a "high," and, of course, the type of acorn they are eating would be responsible for the amount of tannic acid they are ingesting. Naturally, eating white-oak acorns would not stimulate the deer as much as would eating the black-, scrub-, or rock-oak acorns.

A starving white-tailed deer fawn.

I HUNT THE **ridge of mountains that makes up part of the Delaware Water Gap. One Sunday I had the family out for a drive and we went up over the ridge. It looked like winter because all the trees were bare. All the leaves had been eaten off by gypsy moth caterpillars. Oaks are about the only trees that grow on the ridge, with blueberry bushes underneath. My question is this: Will this affect the acorn crop and the deer?** *J. Z., Bangor, Pennsylvania*

I live at the foot of the same ridge of mountains over in New Jersey on the north side of the Delaware Water Gap. I, too, have been up on the ridge a number of times lately, and I have to agree with you, the trees are almost as bare as they are in winter. You can actually hear the caterpillars chewing, and their droppings falling on the dried leaf parts sound like rain.

There will be no acorns this year [1989] because the trees are fighting for their very survival. If we have a hard winter, the deer will be in big trouble because they need the fat that they ordinarily put on their bodies by eating acorns in order to survive. I do not believe the oaks will be killed, even though they have been hit exceedingly hard. Fortunately, we had a very wet spring and the trees were able to add growth and strength before the caterpillars destroyed all the leaves. I have noticed some of the trees trying to put out new leaves now since our area has been sprayed. The trees should be back in good health this coming year because the spraying has been very effective. I see thousands of dead caterpillars clinging to the tree trunks.

Everything in life is a trade-off. Although the trees are bare, the forest floor is lush with greenery. With the canopy of the trees opened up, the sun is flooding the forest floor with light and the vegetation is growing wildly. Anytime there are areas where the trees are dead, the opening up of the canopy will have long-term benefits because it will start a recycling of vegetative growth that should provide good deer food for the next ten years.

T HIS FIREARM SEASON **in Michigan I took a fine seven-point buck. Two days later, after eight inches of new snow, I walked past the area where the deer had been field-dressed. Much to my surprise I found numerous deer tracks, and a deer had actually dug through the snow, recovered a piece of intestine, and chewed on the fatty tissue. Actual bite marks could be seen. The deer shouldn't have been starved at that time of the year (mid-November) as there was ample food in the area. Was that common behavior?** *B. B., Canton, Michigan*

DO DEER EAT **meat? I recently read an article that mentioned that an elk was seen eating a bird. I have never heard of such a thing, and I wonder if deer ever do anything like that.**

P. O., Austin, Texas

Deer are classified as herbivores, meaning that they feed primarily – almost exclusively – on plant material. But, yes, deer do eat meat. There are quite a few records of deer eating fish, dead birds, or other types of meat; however, this is the first time I've heard of deer exhibiting cannibalism.

Almost all does eat meat. After giving birth a doe pulls the afterbirth – the placental sac in which the fawn was encased – from her body and eats it. She doesn't do this because she is a meat eater, although eating the afterbirth helps to stimulate the flow of her colostrum, or "mother's milk." She eats the afterbirth to prevent it from attracting predators to the area. What is little known is that she licks up every drop of amniotic fluid that she can find, licking it up off the ground and off the vegetation. She often will eat the vegetation that it's on. She will do everything in her power to remove every trace of the birth odor.

Once, while in Yellowstone National Park, I videotaped some cow elk

Eating the afterbirth helps stimulate the doe's milk flow and remove signs of the birth.

The shallows of a lake offer food, drink, and a place to cool off.

chewing on baby cottontail rabbits. None of the rabbits were eaten, but five were killed and three of those were chewed up considerably. I believe the elk did it more out of curiosity than hunger, however.

In the revised edition of *The Deer of North America* I tell of a number of instances of deer eating fish. In most instances the deer ate fish that had been caught by fishermen and were lying on the bank or on the ice. One doe was seen in the spring wading into the shallow water of a stream and killing and eating suckers that were migrating upstream to spawn.

The oddest example of food intake involved a two-and-one-half-year-old white-tailed doe that was killed in Herkimer County, New York. Pieces in her stomach proved that she had just eaten a rufous-sided towhee. Undoubtedly, the bird had just been killed somehow and had been found by the deer. The bird had been eaten as carrion, but it had to have been a fresh kill as there was no sign of fly eggs, maggots, or beetles on the feathers or in the meat.

I believe that deer, like many animals, will eat meat when the opportunity presents itself.

M Y FAMILY HAS **a cabin in the Adirondack Mountains of New York. We often see the deer in the summertime feeding in the shallow parts of the lakes, but I don't see them doing this in other areas. Why?** *G. J., Poughkeepsie, New York*

Deer have a tendency to feed more often in wilderness lakes because there is never as much food in wilderness areas as there is in farmland areas. Ordinarily, the lake areas are the only places where sunlight gets down to the ground level. In mature forests the canopy formed by the trees shades out all the low-growing vegetation so there is almost nothing for the deer to feed on.

In the ponds and lakes the deer will eat all sorts of water plants, but they especially relish the gauzy, filamentous type of algae that grows suspended in the water. Algae is a highly nutritious food since it is rich in protein.

Deer also seek refuge in the lakes from the hordes of biting, stinging, bloodsucking insects that plague the wilderness areas in the late spring and early summer.

ARE THERE NATURAL **mineral licks that deer make use of?**

J. Z., Aliquippa, Pennsylvania

Yes, there are a great many natural mineral licks that wild animals know about and use. In addition to salt, some of the other minerals found in such places are calcium, phosphorus, and magnesium. I know of a number of licks that are being used right now.

Some of the licks are so large that they have become historically famous. A number of these sites are place names on our road maps: Lick Creek, Tennessee; Licking River, Kentucky; and Lick Creek, Indiana. Daniel Boone and other pioneers used to boil salt at some of the salt licks in Kentucky.

I have seen huge areas eaten away in some of the western mountains where wild animals have for years been getting the minerals that they instinctively know they need.

MANY TIMES, WHILE **hunting in the Blue Ridge Mountains in the wintertime, I have seen deer eat the leaves of the rhododendron. Are these leaves as good a deer food as the old-timers** claim?

O. E., Roanoke, Virginia

The rhododendron bushes are evergreen and are sometimes eaten by deer in the winter. The leaves contain a poison known as andromeditoxin that is fatal to livestock; however, it is believed that deer can eat the leaves with impunity because they have no gall in their livers.

When you see deer eating rhododendron it is a sign that no other foods are available to them. This plant is a "stuffer" food, having almost no nutrition for the deer. Deer eating rhododendron are usually starving deer.

Deer can reach up to seven feet to browse. They favor twigs less than one-eighth inch in diameter.

I HUNT IN the province of New Brunswick in Canada where there are deer, moose, and hares. When I see twigs that have been browsed, how can I be sure which of the three animals did the browsing, since they all eat the same browse? *B. D., York, Pennsylvania*

That should be no problem. Hares are similar to rodents in that they have four opposing incisor teeth in the front of their mouths. Any browse clipped off by a hare will look as though it had been cut off with pruning shears.

Both the deer and the moose have incisor teeth in just the bottom of their mouths. These lower incisors work against a pad of gristle in the front of the top of the deer's mouth. Because they have no opposing incisors the deer and the moose literally tear each twig loose so that there are always fibrous strands left. That's how you differentiate between twigs eaten by deer and those eaten by hares.

In browsing, a hare will take twigs up to three-sixteenths inch, a deer prefers twigs less than one-eighth inch, while moose feed on twigs up to one-fourth inch. Moose will eat twigs up to three-eights inch and, in times of starvation, deer will eat twigs up to one-fourth inch.

Under normal, nonsnow conditions, hares feed at a height of six to eighteen inches from the ground, a deer from twenty-four to sixty inches, and a moose from forty to eighty inches. In times of starvation a hare may feed up to twenty-two inches by standing on its hind legs, a deer may feed up to eighty-four inches, and a moose up to ten feet. Moose are the only hoofed animals that I have ever seen stand up, straddle a sapling with their front legs, and push the sapling over with their chests and body weight in order to feed on the tops. Many saplings up to three to four inches diameter are broken off by moose in this fashion.

During times of deep snow the hares can feed much higher on the bushes by standing on the snow. Snow seldom packs or crusts hard enough to support a deer's weight because of their sharp hooves. However, the weight of the snow may bend many branches down to within reach of the deer. Moose, because of their great weight, almost never can be supported by the snow but they, too, benefit from snow-bent branches.

I F DEER HAVE **a reduced basic metabolism rate in the winter to prevent starvation as you claim in your book *The Deer of North America*, why do so many deer die of starvation in the early spring?**

T. L., Boston, Massachusetts

What I said was that if there is a gradual decline in temperature, the deer in the northern portion of our country experience a slowdown in their basic metabolism rate (BMR), which is a measurement of the conversion of food to energy. What the deer are doing innately is putting their motors in idle.

An average buck will consume twenty-four hundred to thirty-two hundred calories per day in autumn and perhaps more when he is glutting himself on acorns to increase fat storage on his body. In the winter food of any kind is scarce, nutritious food even more so. To compensate for this shortage the deer's entire system slows down, and at this point it couldn't eat more food even if it were available. The deer loses weight during this period, but even cattle that are fed good, nutritious food will lose 15 to 20 percent of their body weight during this same period.

The deer's activities also slow down as it seeks out the well-protected draws, valleys, swamps, clumps of evergreens, or south-facing slopes. Anything to be out of the wind. Almost all nighttime activity ceases because the deer feeds only during the warmer daylight hours. All of these are heat-conservation measures. The bulk of the nourishment that sustains a deer's life at this point is its own catabolized body and bone-marrow fat.

Photoperiodism triggers a slowdown of the BMR in the fall, and lengthening daylight hours in late winter stimulates an increase. As the deer's BMR increases, its demand for food also increases. If the deer has just come through an exceptionally hard winter, its body reserves may well have been depleted. If new vegetation isn't available for food at this time, the deer may die of starvation before the resurgence of vegetative growth. When a deer loses 33 to 35 percent of its body weight it dies.

I HAVE HUNTED **in the pine woods of East Texas for the past several years on almost every weekend of our deer season. I have taken eleven deer in that time but never a single one, buck or doe, after the first week of December.**

Each year they seem to vanish from the earth after four or five weeks of gun season. I know that they would be moving at night and staying close to cover because of the pressure, but even at night the deer must leave tracks or sign. My hunting partners and I have scoured the lease for tracks, but to no avail. We thought that the deer had moved off the lease, which is two hundred acres of broken pine and hardwood. We questioned friends on other leases and everyone had the same answer to our question: no deer seen, no deer tracks, no deer sign!

What happens to our deer at this time of the year? How can they survive without some movement? Do deer "yard up" in our part of the country? I have read in *Deer & Deer Hunting* that they do this in the north.
                                                           G. C., Sugar Land, Texas

I have pondered over your question for a long time and I'm not sure I have an answer. My first thought was that the deer were moving only at night because of hunting pressure, but you say that a thorough search revealed absolutely no deer sign. Deer just can't live in an area without leaving tracks and scat droppings.

My next thought was that the deer had moved to adjoining land. Deer in my area often leave our lowland areas for the more inaccessible mountain ridges when they are hunted hard. However, you claim that your neighbors weren't finding any deer or deer sign on their land either.

No, your deer would not yard up. Deer up north yard up in areas such as swamps, cedar breaks, and hollows for protection from the frigid winter winds. Deer can stand all the cold in the world, but they can't stand wind. However, your deer are not subject to such extremes.

Your two hundred-acre lease is about one-seventh the area that is a deer's normal home range. The deer must be leaving your lease, in a seasonal food shift, to feed elsewhere. I know that doesn't explain why other hunters on other leases are not seeing deer either, but I can come up with no other answer. If you or your state game biologists can come up with another answer, I'd like to hear about it.

When browsing, deer tear twigs off by clamping their lower incisors against a pad of gristle in the front of the upper jaw.

IRENE VANDERMOLEN

W HY DO DEER feed more before a storm?

J. O., Shreveport, Louisiana

Deer dislike moving in high wind, in snowstorms, or in hard, prolonged rain-storms. If the deer are feeding heavily in the daytime, it is not to take advantage of the light, it is to fill their paunches prior to their remaining sheltered or bedded for extended periods of time during the forthcoming storm.

If you see deer feeding during the daylight hours in late spring, summer, or early fall, you can count on a big storm coming in.

O NE SATURDAY MORNING in December during shotgun season in Massachusetts I stayed on my stand until around nine o'clock when I had the urge to move around and get a little warmer while checking out new hunting grounds. I worked my way up a ridge that paralleled a small brook about four to six feet wide at a distance of about 100 to 150 yards (just out of earshot).

On reaching the limit of where I had planned to go, I became too hot in my wool jacket and decided to take a break. I thought I would cross the brook, hang out for a few minutes, have a snack, and then parallel down the brook while still hunting. I found a perfect log approximately fifty feet from the noisy brook, and assuming that no deer would be around *that* brook, I started to sit down. The exact instant I sat down two deer bolted from their beds under a hemlock tree about seventy-five feet downstream, on my side of the brook. I just couldn't believe that they had bedded down so close to a babbling brook. I have always figured deer rely heavily on their hearing and wouldn't put that defense in jeopardy.

Since they were in a thicket of saplings and pines, no shot could be risked. I took up their trail as best I could on bare ground, but they were long gone. About fifteen minutes later I heard a shot from the direction they had traveled. Maybe I improved the luck of another hunter.

The next Wednesday I again came to a small creek, about one to two feet wide, as I was going to my stand. It had snowed enough to cover the ground a bit, and as I started to cross the creek I noticed fresh clear tracks. I followed the tracks and found that deer had bedded down right up by the creek. Unbelievable!

Facing downstream enables a deer to look out for movement below and still catch the odor of anything moving upstream.

These are my questions: Do deer somehow know that being near running water is safe during the hunting season or do they just end up there from lack of hunting pressure? In the second example, were the deer there because some sort of food was available? Or do you think that deer are just becoming smarter to man's ways?

S. S., Athol, Massachusetts

I think it was just happenstance that the deer were bedded near the brook. You mentioned how warm you got as soon as you moved about because you had a wool jacket on, so although you were cool while standing for several hours, you got hot as soon as you moved. You had on a light wool jacket; the deer had on their heavy winter coats. The temperature along a fast-moving stream will be five to ten degrees or more cooler than the temperature 100 feet or so away from the brook. As the water moves, especially if there is any turbulence, it pulls air currents along with it. Since the water is almost always cooler than the air, except in freezing weather, there is a heat exchange between the water and the air, which also creates air currents. Moving air cools the ambient temperature, which is the principal behind electric fans.

The deer were along that stream because it was cooler for them. Deer are easily stressed during warm spells when they have their winter coats.

If hunting pressure had been severe the deer probably would have sought thicker cover, although you did not say whether the cover was heavy or not. That brookside also may have been the best cover in the area, and it often is because thicker brush grows where it has access to extra water.

A deer's sense of hearing is extremely important, but its sense of smell is paramount. The sounds of your moving about were undoubtedly muffled by the sound of the moving water. However, you said the deer bolted as soon as you crossed the stream and sat down. Those same air currents that made it cooler along the stream also carried your scent directly to the deer. I'm willing to bet that those deer were lying facing downstream so they could detect the motion of anything coming up the stream toward them while they depended on their noses to detect anything above them. In this case that was you, and they were gone.

In the second case you are probably right – there may have been some food that they were feeding on. Although there was snow on the ground, the water would be warmer than the freezing air and, unless the stream was iced over, would usually promote vegetative growth when none other was available. Or the deer could have just gone to the stream for a drink of water.

DO ALL HOOFED **animals chew a cud? Why? Do they all chew it the same number of times?** *L. P., Erie, Pennsylvania*

No, not all hoofed animals chew a cud. All members of deer, bovine, and antelope families chew a cud. The pig, horse, and some other hoofed animals do not.

All of the cud-chewing animals are your basic prey animals – animals that are preyed upon and eaten by the large predators and man. And man is a predator, make no mistake about that. These prey animals are known as ruminants, all having four-chambered stomachs. They were designed in this fashion so that they would be exposed to danger for the shortest possible time each day. While they are feeding they cannot stay hidden but must move about.

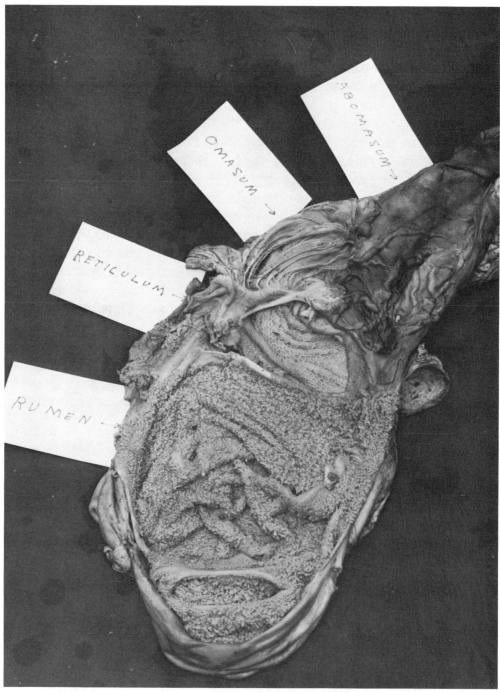

The four compartments of a deer's stomach. From bottom: rumen, reticulum, omasum, and abomasum. The abomasum is the true digestive stomach.

While they are feeding more of their attention is focused on gathering food than on predators. They cannot make as good use of their senses because their senses are helping them to locate their food. If they had to thoroughly masticate their food before swallowing it, they would be exposed to danger for as long as it took them to fill their stomachs. Being ruminants, they are able to just tear their food loose and to swallow it, thus filling up their stomachs in a much shorter period of time. They then retire to some safe spot, where they are hidden, to chew their cuds. According to the species, a piece of material about the size of a large lemon is regurgitated from the rumen, or first compartment of the stomach. This comes up into the animal's mouth and, with a sideways movement of the lower jaw, is ground up by the animal's molars. It is then reswallowed where it goes into the reticulum, then the omasum, on through the abomasum, and then into the intestines.

The various animals masticate their cuds a different number of times and I believe the number of times is determined by the toughness of the vegetation they eat. White-tailed deer chew their cuds on the average of thirty-five to forty-five times, caribou and sheep fifty to sixty times, moose sixty to seventy times, and mountain goats about eighty-five times. The alpine grasses that goats eat are as tough as wire.

YOU CLAIM THAT **white-tailed deer go up on hills to lie down and chew their cuds. In southern New Jersey our deer seek out the lowest ground. Why?** *C. J., Salem, New Jersey*

You have answered your own question. There are no hills in the Pine Barren regions of southern New Jersey. As I have said, the deer will go up on hills, or will seek out the densest cover available, to bed down. The southern New Jersey deer seek out the lowest ground because that is where the swamps and the densest, impenetrable cover will be.

If there are hills, white-tailed bucks will bed down on the tops of them during the daylight hours. This will not hold true in cold, windy weather when the deer will seek out hollows, swamps, and dense stands of evergreens in order to escape from the wind.

Deer seek out hilltops when they are available because during the daylight hours, which are the warmest in any twenty-four hour period, thermals of warm air will rise. Thus, by lying on the tops of the hills, the scent of everything that moves below the deer will be wafted up to them.

In the evening the thermals cease to rise and the air currents reverse themselves, flowing back down the hills. Now the deer leave the hilltops to feed in the valleys below.

If there are no hills in the area, the deer will bed on the level in whatever cover is available. Many bucks escape hunters by bedding in a patch of high grass or brush that the hunters bypass because they thought it too small for a deer to hide in.

WE USE DOGS down here in the South Carolina coastal region to hunt deer because the vegetation is so thick and there is so much flooded ground that a man simply can't get through the brush and water areas. Consequently, during the hunting season our deer spend a lot of time in the water. My friends and I were wondering if the deer ever lie down in water. We would be interested to know if you have ever seen a deer bed down in water. *E. C., Sparta, South Carolina*

I have really racked my memory on this one and I cannot recall ever seeing a deer actually lie down in water. I read in John James Audubon's book on

Deer are strong swimmers when necessary, but like most animals they are more comfortable with their feet on the ground.

mammals that he had seen a deer lie down in water, but I don't recall hearing or reading of anybody else witnessing this occurrence. If Audubon wrote it, then Audubon saw it because he was one of the greatest, most observant field naturalists that this country has ever had. He was an expert on animals as well as birds and he spent much of his lifetime in some of the wildest spots in America.

I did read of a white-tailed buck that was being heavily hunted that jumped into a stream and stood in the water up above his shoulders with his head hidden by the weeds and reeds that hung over the bank down to the water's edge.

This last fall I saw a buck that was greatly overheated after losing a fight with another big buck. This vanquished buck ran from the scene of the fight and entered a small pond. He waded out until the water was up to his shoulders. He stood there gulping air to catch his breath and cooled his heated body in the cold water.

How long do deer sleep? I have a tree stand on private land in Hunterdon County, New Jersey, on the edge of a wooded area that is mostly oak trees. There is an alfalfa field that the deer use quite heavily after it has been mowed. One morning, just as it was getting light, I saw a doe and her two fawns feeding in the field. Around seven o'clock they left the field but walked along the edge of the woods until they were about 150 feet from me. Then they entered the woods and lay down. A distance of 150 feet was too far for me to shoot and there was quite a bit of brush between us, but I could see two of the deer quite plainly. I spent some time watching them through my binoculars. They chewed their cuds but I didn't see them sleep. Twice they got up and moved around a bit, then they lay down again. Just before nine o'clock they got up and moved out of sight. I was glad to see them go because I don't like to move out of my stand when there are deer around. The deer had been out feeding for at least a couple of hours before I saw them, but I didn't ever see them sleep. They do sleep, don't they? *A. K., Hampton, New Jersey*

You pose a couple of good questions. Yes, deer do sleep, but what they do at night I have no way of knowing because I can't see them. What I can tell you is based on many thousands of hours of personal observation.

A question I'd like to have the answer to is "Can deer sleep with their eyes open?" I ask that because they seldom close their eyes for more than ten to twenty seconds at a time. In my lifetime of deer observations I can't recall ever seeing more than three or four deer actually stretch their necks out on the ground and go into a deep sleep. And even then their ears didn't stop moving. The muscles in a deer's ears have to be their most highly developed muscles for their size; they just never stop moving.

Most of the deer I have seen just doze off for ten to twenty seconds; the slightest sound out of the ordinary jerks them wide awake. They apparently are able to screen out the common sounds made by the wind, flowing water, or dropping leaves, but an alarm call of a squirrel, jay, or crow gets their instant attention. The sound of anything walking through the woods, even the sound of another deer, also gets immediate attention.

As I have said, I have seen deer close their eyelids completely for no more than ten to twenty seconds. I have often seen them hold their heads erect and hold that position with their eyes about half closed for three minutes or more, which leads me to believe that they are dozing off even though their eyes are not closed. Except for the three or four instances where the deer actually relaxed, I have never seen them go into a deep sleep.

Although I have seen deer stay in one bed for three or four hours, I have also seen them get up and change their beds several times in that length of time. Many times they move no more than 100 feet and then they lie down again. I don't know why they bothered to get up and move when they stayed in the same immediate area.

You did not mention it but I'm willing to bet that the doe and her fawns did not lie down all facing the same direction. I have noticed that small groups of deer, elk, pronghorn, wild sheep, and goats usually lie down with each individual animal facing a different direction, which makes it more difficult for a predator to sneak up on them. Although all of these animals can see more than 300 degrees of a circle with monocular vision, they also have some overlapping binocular vision and will look directly at anything that disturbs them. They also face a disturbance so that any sound the disturber makes comes into each ear equally, allowing them to pinpoint the source precisely.

I N THE AUGUST 1990 "Rue's Views" you stated that deer do not sleep soundly. Over the years my own observations have affirmed almost all of your views, but I take exception to that one. Twice over the span of my lifetime I have observed deer in the wild sleeping soundly. The first occasion was in the mid 1950s. I had just gotten out of the military and was working for a construction company as a mechanic/ operator of heavy equipment. We were building ammo bunkers for long-term storage and it required large amounts of fill dirt, which was hauled in from a wooded hillside some miles distant.

This particular day, while substituting for the regular front-loader operator, who was ill, I spotted a buck on the far hillside, walking quickly and angling toward me. I was taking a short break so I sat motionless and watched as he made his way to a windfall not seventy yards downhill from me. He curled up like a dog would and lay with his back to the fallen tree trunk, chin on his feet, eyes closed. The time was 2:20 P.M. When I started the engine again he raised his head and watched. An hour later I shut the tractor down and secured it for the day. I walked to the edge and looked for the buck. He was still there looking at me and I carefully avoided making eye contact. I went back to the tractor and climbed up. From that height I could see him. I poured my last cup of coffee as he lay his head back down and went to

A deer bed with the snow scraped away.

sleep. I drank my coffee and watched him for about half an hour. He did not open his eyes or move his ears, and he was still in the same position when I climbed down and left.

My second observation was just a few years ago, soon after I purchased my back forty. I had taken a small buck early in the season and was trying to learn more about the trails and habits of deer in my hunting area.

The south and back sides of my property are bordered by a creek and this particular afternoon I was still-hunting along the bank, looking for prominent points of crossing. I was standing with a big sycamore to my back when I spied a doe on the far hillside. She walked to a brush-pile, crawled under, curled up, and went to sleep. The time was 3:30 P.M. I sat and watched and she slept soundly, not moving at all. I still had about two miles to walk so I left at 4:40 P.M. I did not spare the noise and walked rapidly away. On the far side, from about 200 to 250 yards, I took my last look through my binoculars and she had not moved.

I cannot say how often deer do sleep soundly, but I am firmly convinced that they do, and as soundly as anybody.

R. G., *Newport News, Virginia*

Please note that I stated in my August 1990 column that in my lifetime of studying deer (I started in 1939) I have seen deer go into a deep sleep only three or four times. You say that in your lifetime you have seen deer sleep soundly only twice. You saw it around 1955 and again around 1987, so your average is about the same as mine. Instead of taking exception to my observations, I think we have to agree that soundly sleeping deer are the exception.

In the midfifties incident you evidently were working on government property since you were building ammunition bunkers. On many government properties, and particularly on properties containing ammunition bunkers, no hunting is allowed, so the buck there had a lot less to fear from humans and had evidently become conditioned to the noise of the machinery. You also stated that the buck raised his head each time you started the engine, moved the equipment, or walked about, so I'm not sure just how deep a sleep he was in.

In most areas does are not hunted as heavily as bucks so they are usually less wary than are bucks, especially big bucks.

I did not say that deer don't sleep soundly; I do say that they don't get a chance to do it often. With most wildlife, eternal vigilance is the price of life.

Though he is lying down, this buck is alert and watchful. Deer rarely close their eyes in daylight for more than twenty seconds.

IN THE LAST few years I have heard a lot of conjecture concerning the peak of the white-tailed deer rut. I have hunted extensively in northcentral Georgia for twenty-five years and I know that deer are rutting by late October or early November. This is evidenced by increased activity, scrapes, and the fact that the bucks are running with the does.

The enigma is that some supposedly knowledgeable people just 100 miles west of here (in eastern Alabama) insist that their peak rut is January. Others say the same with respect to the rut in Mississippi and in eastern Texas. I understand that a significant difference in latitude could impact the rut, but different longitudes should have no effect if typography, climate, and plant life are essentially unchanged.

Since the one undeniable constant is the gestation period, and since the vast majority of southern whitetails are said to be born in May, I contend there is no way the peak rut could vary by two months. Also, I

have read game biology texts that indicate that the peak testosterone levels in the bucks occur in November, which would coincide with the peak rut.

S. C., Stone Mountain, Georgia

Basically, the dividing line between the breeding seasons lies between the thirty-second and thirty-third parallel of latitude north. For most of the northern three-quarters of the United States the bulk of the breeding season will be between November 8 and 25, with the peak of the season occurring between the ninth and the twelfth. This can be influenced by factors such as stormy weather and cold. The peak of the 1989 breeding season occurred two to three

Bucks are capable of breeding more than a month before the does come into estrus. In this waiting period a buck will usually check out every doe that comes along.

days earlier, as I had predicted, because August was a dark and stormy month, the rainiest fall on record. A friend of mine in Iowa said that their bucks went absolutely crazy between November 7 and 10. The additional darkness caused by the prolonged storms fooled the deer's pineal gland into thinking the days had actually shortened. The pineal gland is the receptor of the light values accumulated by the deer's eyes. The amount of light received triggers the release of gonadotrophic hormones, which in turn cause the male sex hormone testosterone to be produced. It is the level of testosterone in the buck's system that launches the rutting season. Similar glandular activity in the doe causes her to come into estrus at the same time.

Below the thirty-second to thirty-third parallel the breeding season may be one to two months later. I have just come home from spending two weeks of mid November in Louisiana and Texas. The bucks had made very few rubs, most were totally indifferent to scrapes, there was almost no swelling to their necks, and I saw only one instance of aggression.

A few years ago I saw a number of deer breeding in central Louisiana on January 4, 5, and 6. The photograph of the whitetails breeding in the revised edition of my book *The Deer of North America* was taken at that time.

Other factors, such as elevation, also play a crucial role in determining the timing of estrus and the rut. Although most of the deer in Texas breed in the later period, those on the Edwards Plateau are synchronous with the northern deer because the plateau is several thousand feet higher than the rest of the state.

You are right in saying that the length of the gestation period is a constant, of about 203 to 205 days, and that the vast majority of southern white-tailed fawns are born in May, but only north of the thirty-second to thirty-third parallel. The deer in the more southern regions drop their fawns two months later in July or August.

The key deer on the southernmost tip of Florida are in a truly tropical environment and fawns have been born in every month of the year. However, the peak of their breeding season also occurs in January.

AS I UNDERSTAND **it, the annual rut is largely controlled by day length. (Or is it night length?) In the fall of 1985 in the upper Midwest we had a great deal of overcast and rainy weather. Would that have affected the timing of the rut?** *G. W., Bemidji, Minnesota*

You are correct in stating that the annual rut is determined by photoperiodism, the amount of daylight in a twenty-four-hour period. Although I have seen no

LEN RUE, JR.

Buck tending a doe in estrus. White-tailed bucks pursue does very aggressively during the rut.

scientific data to back up what I am going to say, I am convinced that an excessively overcast fall will cause the onset of the rut to occur earlier than usual. Extensive overcast lessens the amount of light reaching the deer's eyes as effectively as the shorter daylight hours do.

You asked about the fall of 1985. That fall New Jersey had the rainiest October and November on record and those conditions prevailed over most of the northwestern section of the United States. The rutting season and the peak of the rut were ten days earlier than usual. Not only was the rutting season advanced but almost all other occurrences that depended on photoperiodism were also early. I had chickadees, juncoes, and white-throated sparrows come down from the north, to my feeders, earlier than usual as well.

WE LIVE JUST a few miles from town and there are quite a few deer in our area. We have often seen a young six-point buck come out of the woods and chase the old does all over the place, although he never bothered the fawns. Sometimes the fawns would run off when their mother did, but most of the time they just stood and watched the chasing activity. In most cases the old doe would just run around in a big circle and then go back to the area where she had been feeding in the first place.

Is this chasing behavior common among deer? Does a doe ever have any choice in deciding which buck she is going to breed with?

D. P., Tunkhannock, Pennsylvania

Yes, the chasing behavior is one of the main activities engaged in between white-tailed bucks and does during the rutting season.

Bucks are capable of breeding from the time they peel the velvet off their antlers in early September, but no doe is ready to breed at that time. Most does in the northern part of the United States come into their estrus period around

The hard stare is an extremely aggressive posture and scatters the does immediately.

November 10 to 25. However, that fact does not prevent the bucks from being hopeful. Although most bucks concentrate on heavy feeding from September 15 to October 15, in response to an innate mandate that they do so, they seldom pass up a chance to check out every doe that they encounter. Upon seeing a doe the buck lowers his head, extends his neck, and trots quickly at the doe. The doe will either quickly squat and urinate so the buck can check for pheromones or she will dash off. If the doe elects to run off, she adopts an almost sneaking, bent-legged position, which reduces her entire body height by about one-third. She employs this position whether there is any brush to sneak under or not. Her head and neck are also lowered and extended. After using this sneak position for about 100 feet or so she will then straighten up, clamp her tail down tightly, and run off in regular fashion. The buck will usually pressure her until he can get her to urinate.

Usually the largest, dominant buck in any given area will do the bulk of the breeding, and it has been my observation that most does prefer the largest bucks. It is as if they instinctively know that such a mating will provide their offspring with the greatest possibility of surviving by inheriting the best genes. Similarly, men with money have a better chance of getting the beautiful women of their choice than do men without money. The money, in effect, makes such men "larger and stronger" and thus they not only can provide better for the women, they can also provide more for their offspring.

I have concrete proof that some does have a decided preference for a particular buck. I have several deer in captivity that I use for observation in my studies and for the collection of urine. One of my old does disliked my one buck intensely; there was animosity between them at the feeder. When the buck had his antlers he dominated the doe; when he didn't have antlers she tried to dominate him. Just prior to coming into her estrus she stretched the strands on the hog-wire fence and squeezed through the hole. She was bred by a good ten-point buck that had often paced the fence on the outside of the pen. I know that that was the buck that bred her because after being out for her twenty-four-hour breeding cycle she returned to my yard with the big buck following her at a distance. And she did this two years in a row.

I know of another incident where the doe had absolutely no role in choosing the buck, any of the bucks, that bred her. During World War II the Hercules Powder Company had a munitions plant in my home town of Belvidere, New Jersey. When the plant's fence had been erected it had fenced in a number of deer. As no hunting was allowed because of the munitions, the herd increased rapidly and many good bucks were seen inside the fence. One November a doe came over the hill followed by nine bucks. Her mouth was open and her tongue hung out because of her exertions. She could not outrun the bucks and every time she lay down one of the bucks hit her with his antlers or feet and forced her to get up. She got absolutely no respite and in the fifteen to twenty minutes that she was in sight she was mounted by three different bucks. There was no fighting among the bucks. When last seen she was going over another hill, followed by all nine bucks.

I HAVE READ **many articles about rattling antlers, which is supposed to sound like bucks fighting. I have never seen deer fight and neither have any of my hunting buddies, but I have seen some of your photographs showing two bucks fighting. Would you tell me what actually takes place when bucks fight?** *M. M., Harrisburg, Pennsylvania*

Deer fights are not as common as many writers would have you believe. Ordinarily only equal bucks fight; a small buck is not about to take on a big buck. Bucks that share the same area, those that travel together, seldom slug it out in an all-out fight. They are constantly testing one another all year long so that they already have their station in the hierarchy figured out. However, dominance is a constantly fluctuating situation and even the slightest injury may cause the dominant buck to be displaced. If the dominant buck is badly injured, every other buck, including the small ones, will attack him at every opportunity and probably kill him.

In the breeding season deer fight with their antlers. During the rest of the year they fight by striking out with the sharp, cloven hooves on their forefeet. Does always fight that way.

Bucks fight when they expand their home range during the rutting season and encounter bucks of equal size that they have not tested before. They will not fight if they can intimidate a potential rival by bluff, posturing, and threats.

When two strange bucks that are equal in size and antler mass meet, they give each other a "hard stare." This is done with the head held lower than the back, with the chin tucked in so that the antlers project forward. The ears are held back against the neck and the eyes are often rolled upward so that some of the whites show.

If neither buck shows the sign of submission by lowering its head, breaking off eye contact, lowering its body, and slinking off, the threat gestures increase. Still maintaining the hard stare, the bucks erect all the hair on their bodies so that they appear much larger in size. They flick the tongue out of alternate sides of the mouth and up over the muzzle very rapidly. They turn sideways to one another to make sure the rival can see how big and tough they really are. They walk with a very stiff-legged gait, almost as if they were crippled. And they often grunt while circling one another.

If neither buck backs down at this point, a fight is inevitable and the attack happens with unbelievable speed, each buck reacting simultaneously with the other. The bucks crash together, head on, with tons of pressure. The purpose of the buck's blood-engorged neck during the rutting season is to act as a shock absorber so that the neck is not broken during a fight. Once contact is made, each buck strives mightily to push his opponent off his feet. I can always tell, when I look at a photograph, whether the bucks depicted are sparring or really fighting. In a real fight the legs are held wide apart and the entire body is lowered to reduce the center of gravity. The hind legs are extended much farther back than is normal as the bucks try to power-drive each other backwards.

Some fights last only a few seconds and are quickly decided. Others last fifteen minutes or more. In many fights the bucks break off antler tines or even an entire antler. The buck that loses an antler loses the fight as well.

Each buck would like to push his rival backwards and then pull his own head back, breaking contact and trying to slip past his rival's antlers to catch him in the body. It seldom happens. However, one buck is usually just a bit

As the aggressive buck on the left approaches, the other buck drops its head, a signal of submission.

When neither buck submits, a fight is the only way to determine status.

Using their powerful hind legs the bucks try to push each other off their feet.

stronger than his rival and, after contesting with each other, they both know it. When the opportunity presents itself the weaker buck will break contact, whirl about, and dash off at top speed. The victor may chase the vanquished for several hundred yards and then stop. He has proven his point—he is the better buck and both bucks know and acknowledge it.

I WAS DRIVING **down the highway early one morning and saw two deer about one hundred yards from the road. I could not determine their sex from that distance; however, one was mounting the other as if breeding. Can you explain why this would occur in July? Do does mount each other when they are in estrus as do domestic cows? That would still be unusual for this time of year.** *R. H., Westminster, Maryland*

I have seen does attempt to mount other deer as a gesture of dominance, but this was usually during the fall. And I have seen a doe mount another doe who was obviously coming into estrus in November, as domestic cattle do.

I have often seen a buck attempt to mount another buck, usually as a form of dominance. However, last fall I saw a four-point buck attempt to mount an eight-point buck on several occasions. The penis was not extended from its sheath.

A friend of mine saw and photographed a large buck mount another large buck, which stood still for the mounting. Bob could not see whether the penis was out of its sheath or not.

I have seen fawns as young as a month old attempt to mount one another in play in July and August. I have seen young button bucks attempt to mount their dams in October and November.

I have not seen adult deer attempt to mount one another in the month of July as you have just witnessed it. Deer, like humans, are all individuals and do not necessarily follow the norm for the species. Every time I photograph deer I learn something new, as I have just done here with your observation.

W HILE HUNTING IN **Pennsylvania the first week in December one year, I saw something that seemed strange to me. While on stand I saw several deer, maybe ten, run by me. All of these deer were does—at least none of them had antlers. These deer were running very close together, one behind the other. They would run awhile and stop, then take off again. When they stopped, one deer**

Does can also be aggressive. Since they have no antlers, their sharp hooves are their weapons.

attempted to mount another deer in what looked like an attempt to breed.

Could the deer have mounted the other one because of a sudden stop while running in such close formation—not unlike a rear-end collision—or could this have been a buck that had already lost his antlers attempting to breed a doe? I always thought that bucks lost their antlers because of a drop in their testosterone level, thus making them not only incapable of breeding but also uninterested in doing so.

T. J., Grafton, West Virginia

What you saw was not the result of a rear-end collision. I can give several possible explanations for it.

It was early December and the area was Pennsylvania. Although I have

A six-month white-tailed buck tries the dominance kick. Already he is testing himself against the deer around him.

seen a buck shed his antlers as early as November 24 in New Jersey, that was an exceptional case. Usually the deer in Pennsylvania would not shed their antlers that soon because the rut would still be on for at least another week or more. Most Pennsylvania deer shed their antlers between the last of December and the last of January, so it was most unlikely that there were any adult bucks in the group you saw.

What you probably saw was a young button buck trying to mount his mother. This is a very common occurrence; I have seen it many, many times. If the little buck's antlers did not protrude through the skin and were not peeled, he would not be sexually able to breed the doe. But that doesn't mean that he wasn't thinking about it. Most of the times that I have observed a young buck mounting his dam he only went through the motions; his penis was not thrust out of its sheath.

Such dry mountings are also a display of dominance. Many times a button buck will attempt to mount his peers of either sex in an effort to establish dominance over them. I have also observed these same dry mountings by adult bucks, and for the same purpose. If you ever see the hair on an adult buck's hind quarters all scruffed up, it will be the result of another, larger buck mounting the lesser buck to show dominance. I have observed this behavior not only among deer but also among wild sheep, elk, and antelope.

H OW MUCH INBREEDING **takes place among deer, and is this detrimental to the species?** *D. S., Ramapo, New Jersey*

There is actually very little inbreeding among deer, and the little that occurs doesn't harm the species.

Under normal conditions the white-tailed deer has a home range of be-

The swollen neck of a buck during the rut acts as a shock absorber in a fight.

IRENE VANDERMOLEN

tween one to two square miles, depending upon the availability of food. During the breeding season the bucks increase their range up to ten to twelve square miles, or between five and six times what they would normally cover. This also means that the buck is now encountering five and six times more does than he would normally. Twenty deer to the square mile is a good average for deer on good habitat. In some areas it is even higher. In most areas it is lower.

Let's take ten deer to the square mile as being a hypothetical average. In Texas the adult buck/doe ratio is close to fifty/fifty. In my home state of New Jersey it would more likely be eight does to two bucks or even higher in favor of the does. Let's assume that there is a four to one doe/buck ratio. Any buck increasing his range six times, or to twelve square miles, would encounter forty-eight does. Although the buck may be dominant on his home range, he is going to encounter a number of dominant bucks that also have increased their ranges.

Most does are bred within a two-week period at the peak of the breeding season. No one buck can be in all places at one time, nor could he service all of the does in his expanded area. So, although the buck may be dominant in his home range, and related to most of the does, he may not even be on his home range when the related does come into estrus. Bucks from other areas may be there to breed those does while our dominant buck is breeding with the other bucks' relatives. This is not happenstance; it is nature's way of minimizing inbreeding.

DO BUCKS BREED **the does in the same area where they have their primary scrapes? Do they have specific areas for breeding?**

A. J., Endicott, New York

Wild sheep have specific areas where all the males, females, and young gather every year prior to the breeding season. The dominant rams then fight and battle over each individual ewe as she comes into her estrus period. Elk congregate in traditional areas where each dominant bull will gather as many cows into his harem as he is able to keep away from competition. Moose in some sections gather together in breeding groups where the dominant bull will do most of the breeding.

Deer, however, do not have a specific area in which they gather to breed; each buck constantly travels over a greatly expanded breeding range seeking receptive does.

White-tailed buck pawing a scrape. A scrape is a means of informing does of his presence in the area.

A buck may create a number of primary scrapes, since he is anxious to advertise his presence to all of the does and to warn off his competitors. Because a buck expands his home range of from one to two square miles to ten to twelve square miles during the breeding season he may not get back to any particular scrape for three or four days.

It has been observed that when does come into estrus they are as anxious to be bred as the buck is to breed them. At such times they will actively seek out the bucks and they advertise themselves by going to the bucks' primary scrapes.

If the buck is passing through the area and happens to come to his scrape at the same time as the doe, breeding will occur near the scrape. The scrapes are usually made near where the does would normally be so the chances are good, at any time, that breeding may take place near a primary scrape.

Male and female deer do not remain together throughout the year. They will be found together only during the breeding season except when severe winter conditions force them to yard up together. For most whitetails, in most sections of the country, the breeding season occurs during November and the first half of December with the peak of the season occurring from November 10 through November 25.

Throughout most of the year bucks remain in small bachelor groups or remain solitary. Each buck in the bachelor group knows exactly where he stands in the "pecking order," or hierarchy. This hierarchy is a major fact of life with most wildlife. It is usually determined by strength and, in deer, by the size of the antlers. This is nature's way of improving the species.

The larger, stronger deer usually do most of the breeding, and this guarantees that each succeeding generation will be better than the one before it. The hunter who takes a trophy buck can be sure that the genes of that magnificent buck were passed on before he was taken, producing trophy bucks in that area for generations to come so long as nutritious food is available.

Should I hunt **the primary or secondary scrapes?**

T. S., Milwaukee, Wisconsin

By all means hunt the primary scrapes. A deer will make a dozen or more secondary scrapes to every primary scrape. I'm not saying that hunting a secondary scrape is a waste of time, but I would generally consider it to be so. Most secondary scrapes are made by the buck as he walks along, pausing for a few moments to scrape with alternating front feet before continuing on. Since he seldom urinates in the secondary scrapes—they are usually made out in open areas—there is no scent deposited there to attract either the buck that first made the scrape or any other deer to reuse that particular spot. Such scrapes may never be visited again.

Primary scrapes, which are usually made under a tree or bush with low overhanging branches, will have scent rubbed on the overhanging branches from the buck's forehead and preorbital scent glands. Since the buck usually also chews on the overhanging branches, scent from his saliva is also deposited there. The bucks frequently urinate in the primary scrapes, sometimes defecate there, and occasionally masturbate there. The entire area is a treasure

Chewing and rubbing on branches over the primary scrape deposits the buck's scent there.

trove of various scents to the deer. The primary scrapes are meccas to all other deer. These are the scrapes to hunt.

DO WHITE-TAILED DEER **bucks ever make mud wallows like I have seen some of the elk do here in Pennsylvania? Why do the elk do it?** *C. W., Clarion County, Pennsylvania*

No, I have never seen a white-tailed deer make a wallow like elk do. Elk, and sometimes moose, make mud wallows as part of their breeding ritual, but elk do it much more frequently. In making the wallow the elk goes to a wet area or

A whitetail scrape and scent pit.

spring seep and, utilizing both his antlers and his feet, tears the turf apart. In doing this he seems to work himself into a frenzy as he uses his antlers to throw the sod ten to twenty feet away. The water is quickly churned to mud by his feet. He will then urinate and sometimes masturbate in the wallow. He then either paws this mixture over his body or else he lies down and rolls in it, plastering the mud and goo all over his body. When he is thoroughly coated, he leaves. When the breeze is in my favor I can smell a coated bull elk for quite a distance, but it isn't an offensive smell. I suppose he thinks it makes him irresistible to the cows. The red stag of Europe goes through the exact same ritual.

The closest thing that a white-tailed deer will do is paw his scrape, in which he also urinates and sometimes masturbates. However, the buck's

Masturbation is the way a buck relieves sexual frustration.

scrape is made to attract estrous does to the area and to advertise the buck's presence in that particular area. The elk's wallowing is to announce his personal appearance to the cows, and not to a particular area.

I HAVE READ in your book *The Deer of North America* that does come into estrus every twenty-eight days or so, and if they are not bred in that twenty-four- to twenty-eight-hour period, they go out of estrus and come back into their heat period twenty-eight days later. You also state that for most of the northern half of the United States the peak of the breeding period is between November 10 and November 25. My question is this: Would it pay to concentrate on scrape hunting to coin-

cide with the does' estrus cycles? For example, would the scrapes be more productive from November 10 to 25 and again from December 8 to 20 than they would be in between? *T. N., Roanoke, Virginia*

Your reasoning is good, but I truthfully don't think it will make that much of a difference.

First, and foremost, a scrape is the buck's way of advertising his presence; it is primarily the male's way of letting the does know that he is available, and it also serves as a warning, or notification, of his presence to other males.

It is known that does coming into estrus become exceedingly agitated and actively seek out the bucks. I have seen three does urinate in buck's scrapes, but I have not seen a doe ever paw in a scrape, as the bucks almost always do. The does try to attract the bucks since they are as anxious to be bred as the bucks are to breed them.

It is true that most does are bred in the time period I have stated; the records kept by many of the various game research departments have proven this. So theoretically there would be, or could be, increased activity by the does at the scrapes during the two time periods that you mention.

A secondary scrape is merely a place where a buck has pawed the ground a few times; scent is seldom deposited there.

However, although most of the does are bred during that two-week period, many of the largest adult does breed before that time and any of the first-year fawns that are developed enough to be able to breed will do so in December. Deer are like humans, they don't all develop simultaneously. Consequently, although the bulk of the does are bred between November 10 and 25, there are some does in any given area that are probably in estrus from October 25 right on through until December 25.

IS IT POSSIBLE **to tell when a doe is about to come into her heat period?**
C. K., Gary, Indiana

Yes. If you are able to examine the doe at close quarters, you can see that her vaginal area is swollen. Under normal conditions a doe's vagina is little more than a split. Prior to estrus the lips surrounding the opening swell.

Even from a distance the possibility of telling if a doe is approaching estrus is possible. Just prior to estrus does become much more high-strung, nervous, and move about much more. The key, however, is that they urinate much more frequently at that time. The urine and its endocrine pheromones are the doe's way of advertising to the bucks that she is ready for copulation.

IS IT NORMAL **behavior for a doe in heat, and standing upwind of a scrape, to vocalize her presence? I witnessed a doe vocalizing her presence by making a sound similar to that which a person would make gasping for air or wheezing. She made the sound every three to four seconds for one solid hour!**

She also lowered her head until it was three or four inches from the ground and stood absolutely motionless for periods of ten minutes, fifteen minutes, and thirty minutes.

She was as far as twenty yards away from me and as close as eight yards. (I was in a tree stand.) I know that she was healthy and in heat — her hock glands were black and, once behind me, she was certainly ripe to my nose! *J. B., Montgomery, Alabama*

I have never heard a doe grunting that sounded like a person gasping for air. However, because of my extreme deafness, and in spite of the fact that I wear

An estrous doe is as anxious to be bred
as the bucks are to breed her.

two powerful hearing aids, I miss many, many sounds in the out-of-doors.

I have heard, in fact I recorded it on tape, a doe grunt softly to her fawns. This sound was very similar to the grunt that bucks make but was much softer in volume.

It is a well-known fact that just prior to coming into estrus a doe becomes extremely nervous and actively seeks out the buck's scrape. I have not seen a doe in estrus stand still for any length of time; the ones I have observed were on the go almost constantly. Researchers have noted that a doe coming into estrus increases her activity twenty-eight times what would be normal. So I can't explain why the doe you so carefully observed did stand for the length of time, or in the position, that she did. The fact that the hock, or tarsal, glands were so black indicates the increased urination that precedes, and occurs during, estrus.

It was also interesting that you mentioned you could smell the doe when she was upwind from you. I have often been able to detect bucks by their odor.

I'M RESPONDING TO a question in the December 1988 issue of *Deer & Deer Hunting* about a doe vocalizing over a scrape. You wanted feedback from other readers about this.

It was opening day of the 1985 Wisconsin gun season. It was just starting to get light out when I saw a deer coming from the bottom next to a creek, heading directly for a scrape I was sitting by. At about forty yards from the scrape the deer began to grunt, so I figured it for a buck. I was wrong. I sat about twenty to thirty yards away from the scrape and watched an adult doe urinate in the scrape and grunt like a buck for almost ten minutes before slowly walking away. Five minutes later a buck came off the opposite hill, but he spotted me so he didn't follow the doe.

I have also heard the soft grunt of a doe calling her fawns.

T. H., Blanchardville, Wisconsin

Your comments are most appreciated and really very helpful. In a conversation I had with Larry Marchinton he commented that he had seen does urinate in a scrape on five different occasions. I have seen it happen only three times. The does I saw did not paw in the scrape; they just walked into the scrape, put their tarsal, or hock, glands together, and urinated on the glands with the urine running down into the scrape.

You did not mention that the doe you watched pawed in the scrape, so I assumed that she did not.

I am also interested in your comment that the doe grunted like a buck. The does I have heard grunted on a higher pitch, not as deep as the bucks do.

I've LISTENED TO **every tape and watched every video sold, and I've heard white-tailed does in my area make a sound unlike any sound on any of the tapes. It's hard to imitate the sound on paper, but I can equate it to a string being plucked on an acoustic guitar, then the pitch being slightly raised by tightening the tuner. I've heard this when one deer was trying to keep up with other deer. When the trailing deer made the sound the lead animal(s) would stop and wait. I've tried the imitation on deer that I've routed, and they have stopped and allowed me to approach to within about fifty yards.**

The noise is quite unusual. I would never have guessed that a deer would make such a noise. Are you familiar with this sound? What could it mean? I'm under the impression that only does make the sound, since I've never heard a buck make it. Do bucks make it also?

J. A., Glen Dale, West Virginia

No, I have never heard a doe make the sound you describe. I have on a number of occasions heard bucks just prior to fighting emit a high-pitched whine. That whine sounded to me as if it expressed contained fury. It was an angry sound, a little higher than the squealing of fighting horses. I can't begin to imitate the sound because my voice just can't get that high. That could be the same sound you heard. As far as I can discover, no researcher has heard, or at least none has written about, the whining sound that I heard. The difference in the purposes for the sounds that we each heard probably means that the sound was different also.

I am fascinated by the intense interest in the grunt-tending call being used today. Perhaps someone will soon market a call making the sound you heard. We are gaining in deer knowledge by leaps and bounds.

I LIVE IN **Wayne County, West Virginia. The deer in my area do not snort when they are alarmed. Farther north in Braxton County there are a lot more deer and they do snort. Why do they do it up north and not in my area?**   *D. P., Dunlow, West Virginia*

Deer will snort whenever they are alarmed wherever they are found. However, if deer are scarce in your county, they may snort a lot less because there are no other deer to alert in the area. Or, because they are scarce your chances of hearing them are greatly lessened.

Deer are herd, or communal, animals and snorting is done primarily to alert all other members of the herd to potential danger. Naturally, the more deer in any given area, the more often you will hear them snort. But even a lone deer will snort; it is an instinctive reaction to a threatening situation. You may not have heard them but the deer in your area do snort.

I LIVE IN a part of West Virginia where there is a very low deer population. However, I have found several rubs and during turkey season I found a nice shed antler. If a big buck lives in an area where there

Tree rubbed by rutting buck.

are just a couple of does around, will he make scrapes during rutting season and stay in that area, will he stay and not make scrapes, or will he leave to look for more does or other deer?

D. N., Powellton, West Virginia

Finding a nice shed antler proves that you have a nice buck in your neighborhood. Having a good buck in the area means that there have to be does there, as well. Perhaps more than you suspect. If the ratio of does to the one good buck in the area is high, the buck may not make as many rubs and scrapes as he would if he had more competition.

We live in a world of advertising, and so do wildlife. Scrapes and rubs are forms of advertising, plain and simple. The buck that has a number of does to breed, and no competition, doesn't need to spend his time advertising.

Your buck will have a home range of one to two square miles during most of the year, but will increase that range to ten to twelve square miles during the rutting season. So, the buck in your area probably will go out of your area and will be making scrapes and rubs where you don't see them but where he might be encountering more competition in the form of rival bucks.

ALTHOUGH I LIVE in the northern part of our state I do most of my hunting in the southern part because there are bigger-racked bucks there. I haven't shot a monster buck yet, but I'm trying. And I'm sure that there are big bucks where I hunt because I find rubs that are blazed on trees up to six inches in diameter. In your book *The Deer of North America* you stated that although any buck can make a rub on any size sapling or tree, only big bucks make rubs on big trees. Just recently I read where they now believe that the rubs are also a visual sign. Can you give me some more information on buck rubs? Am I right in continuing to hunt the area I do because of the many large buck rubs that I see there?

C. H., Wheeling, West Virginia

When a buck's antlers are growing he does everything in his power to keep from hitting them against anything because before they harden they are very easily damaged. Antlers are generally full grown between the first and the middle of August, when they begin to solidify. Usually between September 5 and 10 the velvet has dried and the buck rubs it from his antlers. All of this is done in response to the increased level of the male sex hormone testosterone that is now coursing through the buck's system. To take the velvet off, the buck

After rubbing his antlers on a tree, a buck deposits scent from his forehead glands there. Most rubs are made by the more dominant bucks.

makes the first rubs of the season. These first rubbings are not the white-scarring rubs that will be made later. The first rubs are to remove the velvet; the later ones are to advertise the buck's identity, presence, and status.

I have seen individual bucks make as many as ten to twelve rubs a day. Contrary to what is generally believed, when a buck makes the bright, white rubs he doesn't do it with his antler tines, he does it with the heavily corrugated ridges, known as perlation, on the base and burr of his antlers. Using this perlation the buck actually grates the bark from the tree as if using a vegetable shredder. He removes the bark in long strings, which he most frequently eats, particularly the cambium, or inner bark.

After grating off the bark the buck will then personalize the white debarked area with scent from his forehead scent glands. The buck is thus serving notice to the world, and to all the other deer, who he is, where he is, and how regal his status is. The more dominant the buck, the more active are his forehead glands in producing the scent that he deposits on the rub.

Yes, the rubs are visual. They get our attention because the whitened, rubbed areas stand out against the other trees. They also get the attention of all the other deer.

In areas where an old field is being taken over by brush we often have uniform stands of hundreds of equal-aged aspen, birches, or sumac. In some of these stands it is not unusual to see forty or fifty buck rubs. Although the bucks seldom rub the same sapling twice, they will use the same stand of saplings year after year.

Most of the rubs will be made by the older, larger, more dominant bucks. Yearling bucks make very few rubs. They usually lack the perlation at the base of their antlers that comes with age, and their forehead scent glands are not nearly as active. Since they do very little of the breeding, they have little need to advertise their presence. If they do make rubs, it is usually much later in the season, particularly if some of the dominant bucks have been harvested by hunters, upsetting the deer's social status.

MAINE NOW HAS **a lot of moose. When we hunt up there how can we tell the difference between a buck rub and a moose rub?**

C. S., Sayreville, New Jersey

Usually a moose will rub on three- to four-inch or larger saplings while most deer prefer saplings of one and one-half to two inches in diameter. Occasionally a really large buck will rub a sapling that is four, five, or six inches and that may be confusing. In that case I would go by the height of the rub. The average white-tailed buck stands thirty-six to forty inches high at the shoulder and most of the rubs will be made eighteen to thirty inches above the ground. The average Maine moose will stand about seventy-two inches high at the shoulder and will make most of the rubs thirty-six to forty-eight inches or higher above the ground.

I HAVE JUST **come in from walking through the woods looking for shed antlers near my home on the outskirts of Sussex, New Jersey, and I just came across the biggest deer rub I have ever seen. I read in your book *The Deer of North America* that there is a definite correlation between the size of the tree rubbed and the deer that did the rubbing. The deer that did that rubbing must have been a monster buck because he had rubbed all the bark off a tree around four to five inches in diameter. And that buck had every piece of bark rubbed off the tree from about six inches above ground level to about five feet above the ground. That's**

the highest I've ever seen. I hunt this area every fall with both bow and gun and I never saw a buck rub on a tree that big before. Could this mean that a really big buck has moved into the area since the hunting season?
F. O., Sussex, New Jersey

I'm sorry to disillusion you about that big buck, but I don't believe that what you saw was a buck rub at all.

You said that you were out looking for shed antlers so I assume that you were in the woods in February or March. At least that's the time I look for antlers. You hadn't seen a rub like that in the hunting season because it wasn't a rub. I'm sure that what you saw was a young tree that had been stripped of its bark by hungry deer. Here in New Jersey we just don't have enough food to feed the number of deer that we have in the state. That's why New Jersey allows a hunter to take twenty-one deer each year.

A couple of things you said tend to confirm that the tree was peeled by hungry deer. The first was the time that you saw it, which was in late winter. The second was that the peeling was done up to a height of five feet. A white-tailed buck couldn't possibly rub a tree that high. It would take an elk to reach such a height.

I want you to go back and look very closely at that tree and look for grooves in the tree trunk made by the deer's lower incisor teeth. Because deer have no teeth in front in the top of their mouths they have to scrape up the tree to peel off the bark. In fact, no matter what food they are eating, whether it is dried corn on a cob, a fallen apple, or even browse, deer always eat with an undercutting motion of the jaws. Not having upper teeth, they cannot eat in any other fashion. And those incisor teeth marks will show.

There is a better-than-average chance that the bark was peeled off and eaten by a doe because we have far more adult does than adult bucks in New Jersey.

I can usually quite accurately estimate the weight of a beaver from the grooves left on a stump that it has cut. I do not see that much size difference in the incisor teeth of deer.

I would be interested in knowing the kind of tree that was peeled. I have seen a number of trees that have been peeled for their bark and most of the time they were young elms. This really surprised me because elm leaves are not a favored food of the deer since they have a higher than normal amount of tannic acid in the leaf, which makes them slightly bitter to the taste. I always figured that there would also be tannic acid in the bark. However, elm bark does peel very easily and perhaps deer eat it because it is easily obtained.

WHAT IS THE **perfect buck/doe ratio?**   *T. W., Roanoke, Virginia*

That depends, I suppose, on whether you are a buck or a doe. I am sure that the bucks like the ratio of eight to ten adult does to one adult buck, as we have it here in New Jersey, particularly during the rutting season. The more even the ratio, as in our southern states, and Texas in particular, the more competition there is between the adult bucks for the privilege of breeding. The more even the ratio, the more competition, the more scrapes the bucks make, and the more they respond to deer calls and to rattling antlers.

In most sections of the country the buck/doe ratio is about 106 to 100 at birth. From that time on the ratio tips heavily in favor of the does. Mortality is

The fewer does there are for every buck during breeding season, the more the bucks have to compete to pass on their genes.

higher among buck fawns than it is among doe fawns. The bucks that do grow up are more heavily hunted, even in areas where either sex can be hunted. Most hunters prefer to shoot a buck than a doe because of the buck's trophy value, no matter what size the antlers are.

Bucks from the time they are born are more adventuresome than does and this makes them more susceptible to injury and predation. Bucks travel much farther than does at most times of the year, but five to six times farther during the rutting season. This exposes most of them to more danger from accidents, to being struck by automobiles, and to being shot. Fighting, too, takes its toll. Even though most deer do not get injured in fighting, some do.

A buck is perfectly capable of breeding eight to ten does in a season, and probably more. However, an ideal ratio from game managers' viewpoints would be one adult buck to each five or six does on the average, or one to one if managing for trophy bucks.

HOW MANY ADULT **bucks are usually found in a herd of deer? I hunt the northern peninsula here in Michigan and I see far more does than I do either bucks or fawns.** *B. B., Detroit, Michigan*

Under ordinary circumstances the sex ratios of most animals at birth run about fifty/fifty. With deer the ratios are usually a little higher in the bucks' favor because the mortality rate for buck fawns is higher than it is for does.

Different circumstances further alter the deer's birth rates. It has been found that when a deer population increases to the point that their range is being destroyed the does give birth to more male fawns. Thus, the does getting poor nutrition have a preponderance of bucks. Conversely it has been found that does getting sufficient, or superior, nutrition will give birth to more female fawns. These situations have been proven, and it may be nature's way of reducing or increasing the deer's overall population in an attempt to keep it in balance with the range's food production.

It has also been found that because of poor nutrition, on a range that is overpopulated, the does will breed later than is normal. Does that breed late in their breeding period also give birth to more male than female fawns.

According to the latest figures that I have the gun-hunting season in northern Michigan is primarily a bucks-only season. Under a special permit arrangement some does and fawns are harvested. Whenever a bucks-only season is in force it throws the sex composition of the herd entirely out of whack. Even where an either-sex season is the norm there is still a reluctance on the part of many hunters to take a doe. The harvest of does in an either-sex season usually runs at about 40 percent.

Currently in Michigan the composition of your herd is approximately 15 percent adult or legal bucks, 50 percent does, and 35 percent fawns.

In my home state of New Jersey the composition is more likely 10 percent adult bucks, 55 percent does, and 35 percent fawns. Both our archery and black-powder seasons allow either sex to be taken, our regular season allows bucks with three-inch or longer antlers only, and our antlerless season is primarily for a designated doe reduction on specific game management areas. In spite of the best attempts at game management—and New Jersey is doing a fine job of it—we still have far more does than we do adult bucks and fawns.

DO YOU THINK **that trophy bucks have different habits than do the rest of the deer?**
W. B., Peoria, Illinois

Yes, that's how they got to be trophy bucks. Most bucks are killed when they are between eighteen and thirty months of age. The bucks that have been shot at and survived, and have learned by the experience, have the possibility of becoming trophy bucks.

Research has shown that most deer escape from hunters by lying low, staying hidden, and not moving around at all during daylight hours. These are the deer that hide in the high grass that grows under the one tree in an otherwise bare field. These are the deer that hide behind a huge boulder just fifty feet from a well-traveled road. These are the deer that have learned to hide in all sorts of places where hunters don't look because "no buck could hide there." These are the deer that have learned that their coats are good camouflage. They have learned not to get so nervous that they break out of cover. They have also learned that when they do have to break to wait until absolutely the last moment and then to get out of the area at high speed and to put every obstacle possible between themselves and the hunter.

Do I actually believe that deer are capable of learning? You bet I do. We don't do ourselves or wildlife justice when we say that they can only react to any given situation. I have lived too intimately with wildlife to believe such nonsense. I'm not being anthropomorphic when I say that most wildlife has the capacity to learn beyond instinct. A trophy buck didn't get to be a trophy buck by accident; he got that way by being smart.

Why hunters aren't likely to see this ten-point white-tailed buck.

Bucks that hide and remain motionless have the best chance of survival.

Deer can remember things like where the holes are in a fence. But why they crawl under when there is no hole, rather than jumping over, is a mystery.

D

O DEER HAVE **good memories? Do they remember being shot at?**

B. L., Indianapolis, Indiana

If you mean do deer remember where a hole in the fence is, then the answer is yes. Deer remember where every apple or white oak tree is in their area. This can be seen by the directness of their travels when they go to feed. They don't just stumble on these trees in their travels; they know where they are, know when they will produce food, and go directly to them.

Unless a deer is hit when shot at it doesn't connect the twang of a bow or the discharge of a firearm with injury. Deer do not think of the possibility of death. We humans may think about or dwell on the thoughts of death; wildlife concentrates on living. Most deer pay no attention to the sound of a shot unless it is very close. Deer have as much trouble locating the source of a single shot as we humans do. We usually need two or more shots to focus on the point of origin, and so do the deer.

If the deer have been shot at and missed, they may bolt from the area but they will not avoid it in the future. If they detect human scent three or four days in succession in the same spot, they may avoid the area whether they have been shot at or not.

THERE HAVE BEEN **times when the wind has been in my favor, I wasn't moving, and still the deer seemed to "feel" my presence. What do you think about that?**   *C. T., Butler, New Jersey*

Yes, I believe that the deer can "feel" our presence. I have said for many years that we will not thoroughly understand communication among wildlife until we understand psychic phenomena. All of us humans have experienced the sensation of "feeling" the presence of something—a person or an impending danger—before our regular senses detected it. If anyone claims not to have had the experience, it is probably because he paid no attention to the sensation or disregarded the feelings that were engendered.

Our ancestors were more in tune with what went on around them. Their survival depended on their sensory and extrasensory awareness.

The deer's survival, like that of our ancestors, depends on the use of all its faculties.

IS IT TRUE **that only a buck runs with his tail erect and is he always the first in line while running?**   *D. P., Dunlow, West Virginia*

Artists usually depict a buck dashing off with his tail erect up over his back. Some bucks do this, some don't. The tail-raising is an individual characteristic that is often altered by circumstances. Some bucks almost always raise their tails, others almost never do.

If a buck is alert but not frightened, he may raise his tail. At such times the hair of the tail can be flared out to a width of eight to eleven inches. If the buck is frightened, he may clamp his tail down and turn his rump hair inward until almost no white is visible.

White-tailed does almost always run with their tails up, their rump hair flared outward, and the tail bobbing loosely from side to side. It's the doe's

Whether or not a buck raises his tail while running seems to be an individual preference.

bouncy, bobbing white tail that her fawns follow as she dashes off through the dark forest on a dark night.

Deer can run at speeds of over forty miles per hour. When a deer is running it has no opportunity to use any of its tremendously well-developed senses of smell, hearing, or sight. It is at a complete disadvantage and the deer knows it. Thus, the deer runs no farther than it has to, which is usually to the nearest copse of dense cover, and there the deer stops.

It may stop completely and watch its back trail or it may cautiously slink on to a better hiding place, but it will do it at its own pace and will take advantage of the wind and every bit of available cover.

No buck is about to stick his neck out when he doesn't have to. In times of danger the buck is usually the last deer in the line. If there are three bucks with the herd, the smallest buck will usually be the first, with the biggest buck bringing up the rear. That's how he got to be big and old—by not taking any chances. The buck you see running at the end of the line may be the only buck with the herd but if there are more than one, each succeeding buck will usually be larger than the one before it.

A clamped-down tail would certainly be less visible to a predator or hunter.

IN YOUR BOOK *The Deer of North America* I read that the doe has a birthing territory and that is the only time that deer have a territory. You said that a pair of fawns will be separated by their mother to reduce predation. How do the does get their fawns to go where they want them to? You also said that fawns usually remain hidden for the first eight to ten days; after that time they follow after the doe and then she no longer defends her territory. Will she still put the fawns where she wants them after she gives up her territory?

O. B., Baltimore, Maryland

As soon after being born as the fawns are able to walk, the doe leads them away from the spot where she actually gave birth. She wants to get them away from where the amniotic fluid, blood, and afterbirth have stained the earth. Such odors attract predators.

I have actually witnessed a doe force her fawn to lie down by pushing on its back with one of her forefeet. I'm not sure how it is generally done, but I do know that the fawns are usually widely separated for the first week or so.

A five-minute-old fawn tries to balance on his wobbly legs. The spike buck may be the doe's previous-year fawn.

After the fawns are big enough to follow after the doe they will bed down in the same general area that she is using. The fawns will select their own actual site and two factors seem to determine just where that spot will be.

Protective cover is of the greatest importance to the fawns and I have watched many of them seek out the thickest cover in the immediate area. I have watched fawns sneak in and virtually disappear by hiding beneath the protective cover of bracken ferns.

The second most important factor determining their bedding sites will be ambient temperature. If the day is cool or cold, the fawns will seek out the heaviest cover where the sun will be able to warm the area. If the day is hot, the fawns will seek the protective cover that will also allow for the greatest amount of cooling shade.

I am constantly amazed how the fawns almost always make the best of each situation.

The doe leads the fawn
away from the birth area
as soon as it can walk.

WE HAVE A **springer spaniel bitch that just had a very difficult time giving birth to her puppies. We had to take her to a vet and have them delivered by Caesarean section. My wife and I were talking about this and wondered what would happen if a doe had a fawn that was turned so that it couldn't be born in the normal position.**   *P. O., Erie, Pennsylvania*

The young of most animals are born head first. Fawns, calves, colts, and so forth are born in a "diving" position with their front feet extended forward beyond the head. When the doe is ready to give birth her vagina dilates (stretches) to accommodate the fawn's large size. The doe is usually lying down and helping, by squeezing, to push the fawn from her body. The hooves of the front feet slide out first, then the head, neck, and shoulders. The length of time that this requires depends upon whether this is the first time the doe has given birth and the extent to which she has dilated. It ordinarily takes between twenty to thirty minutes for a fawn to be born. In the case of twins the second fawn takes far less time than the first because the passageway has already been prepared.

If the fawn should be turned so that it is trying to come out rump first, it would be known as a breech birth. If this should happen in the wild to a doe, she would die.

A single fawn is usually more difficult to deliver than twins because of its larger size.

The front legs are beginning to emerge.

The doe helps push the fawn out by squeezing mightily.

Finally the hind legs slip through.

The fawn, only a few seconds old.

Though exhausted from the delivery, the doe begins the work of cleaning her young at once to remove the birthing odor. Predators could be lurking nearby.

The fawn has found its source of nourishment.

Only thirteen minutes old, the fawn attempts to stand.

Mother encourages his first shaky steps.

At twenty minutes old the fawn is clean, fed, and ready to investigate the world.

I have witnessed the birth of a white-tailed fawn on a number of occasions, but have only been able to photograph it twice.

The first occasion was an easy birth since the doe had given birth before. She had dilated sufficiently and she dropped her twin fawns within twenty minutes of each other. I never heard her make a vocal sound.

The second birth was a difficult one. The doe was young and this was her first birthing. She was inexperienced, single fawns are usually larger than either of a set of twins, she had not dilated sufficiently, and she was in pain. She moaned, she groaned, she strained mightily. The fawn's feet would begin to protrude from her vagina only to slip back in when she jumped to her feet to see if it was born yet. It was a difficult birthing that took over five hours.

Accomplishing two things
at once: a doe cleans
her fawn as it nurses.

In the daytime deer prefer to bed down on a hilltop where
the rising air currents enable them to scent everything below.

The hard stare is the first sign of aggression.

If neither buck backs down, a fight is necessary to prove which is the stronger. The objective is to push the opposing buck off his feet.

The subordinate buck may give way without a fight. One buck mounting another is a sign of dominance.

During the rutting season, the buck advertises his presence by making scrapes. He chews on the branches above a scrape to deposit scent from his saliva there.

A buck licking the vagina of an estrous doe.

When a buck makes
a rub, he uses the
ridges on the base
and burr of his antlers.
A rub is another way
of proclaiming his
presence in the area.

The bark loosened
when making the rub
does not go to waste.

Does and bucks associate with each other only during the breeding season, or when severe winters force them to yard up together.

Most of the year bucks remain solitary or gather in small bachelor groups.

In a normal birth, the
front hooves of the
fawn emerge first,
then the head, then
the rest of the body.

This fawn is three
minutes old. Soon the
doe will eat the
afterbirth and lick up
the amniotic fluid so
that they do not
attract predators.

LEN RUE, JR.

Most fawns north of the thirtieth parallel are born in May or June. This gives them plenty of time to build up strength and fat reserves for the winter.

A doe drives her yearling young away just before giving birth to her new fawns.

Antler growth begins in early spring. When the days begin to shorten, testosterone production increases and causes the antlers to solidify and the velvet to loosen.

An eight-point buck and a button buck.

Flehmening, or lip-curling, enables a deer to trap scent molecules on the moist lining of the nostrils. Moist surfaces allow odors to stick better and forewarn the deer of possible danger.

When deer nervously stamp their feet a secretion from the interdigital glands is deposited on the ground. The scent of this secretion serves as a warning signal to other deer.

LEN RUE, JR.

When a deer is running it cannot sense what is going on around it. That is why deer usually run to the nearest available cover and stop.

White-tailed does almost always run with their tails up so that their fawns can easily follow them. Bucks are more unpredictable; sometimes they clamp their tails down when running and almost no white is visible.

LEN RUE, JR.

When deer groom each
other it is usually
around the head area,
which is the hardest
place for the deer
to reach on itself.

A deer facing downstream is in an advantageous position: it can see anything coming
up the stream toward it and scent anything above it.

The breeding season usually peaks in mid-November north of the thirtieth parallel. Stormy weather, however, can bring it on sooner because the decreased amount of daylight triggers earlier production of testosterone.

Deer play far more than most people suspect. Sometimes they run in water just to see it splash.

Water is a good source of food and a refuge in summer from heat and biting insects.

White-tailed bucks on
a frosty morning.

MARK WILSON

If white-tailed deer are threatened, they can run very quickly — over forty miles per hour. In times of danger the largest buck is usually at the end of the line.

In the evening the air currents flow downhill, so deer go to low-lying areas to feed.

LEN RUE, JR.

HOW SOON AFTER a fawn is born can it survive on its own if its mother is killed?
G. M., Bangor, Pennsylvania

Fawns at about three weeks of age usually start to sample whatever vegetation their mother is eating. At four weeks they begin to drink some water, although they still get most of their liquid requirements filled by their mothers' milk. Fawns are usually weaned when they are four to five months old but research has shown that they are dependent on milk until they are at least three months old. If fawns in the wild are orphaned after three months of age, they probably can survive. If orphaned before three months, they undoubtedly would die.

White-tailed doe letting a seven-month fawn nurse.

Licking another buck's forehead scent glands is stimulating, particularly during the rut.

MY UNCLE HAS a small farm in the southern part of Ohio. I have had good luck bow-hunting there and have several permanent tree stands that I use. One of the stands is at the edge of the woods, bordering an old apple orchard. Once, while I was in this particular stand, I noticed a four-point and an eight-point buck come into the far end of the orchard. They were much too far for a shot so I just sat and watched them. After sniffing around among the leaves and eating some of the fallen apples one buck began to lick the head of the other buck. A short time later the buck being licked also licked the first buck. Just what were they doing, and why? It was the first time I had ever seen deer do this. *C. O., Youngstown, Ohio*

What you witnessed is known as mutual grooming and is a rather common occurrence, not just among the bucks but among all deer. They do this to accomplish a number of things.

Yearling deer are driven away by the mother just prior to her giving birth to her new fawns. At that time a number of the young bucks may band together in a bachelor herd or, as often happens, they may be permitted to join

A buck will even rub his own scent on a stick . . . LEN RUE, JR.

. . . and lick it off.

the company of an older buck. The pair, and sometimes there may be three or four individuals, become constant companions, doing everything together. They reinforce this bonding by mutually grooming each other, which is what you probably witnessed.

When two deer lick each other it is usually around the head area, and quite frequently they are removing ticks from each other. It is the only spot that the deer can't reach on itself. A deer can scratch itself around the head with its hoof but it can't pull ticks off there.

I have also noticed that when two bucks groom each other in October, November, and December they concentrate their licking on the area just in front of and behind the antlers. This is where the deer's forehead scent glands are located. Deer are stimulated by the scent from these glands. I have observed a buck rubbing a stick on these glands and then licking it off. I have seen other bucks and does lick the same stick. The scent from these glands attracts all deer—bucks and does—so that when these glands are most active, during the rutting season, bucks mutually groom each other there frequently.

I AM WRITING **in regard to an article on deer walking on just their forelegs that you printed in the December 1987 issue of** *Deer & Deer Hunting*.

One morning in early November I noticed some whitetails eating in the field behind our house in southern Michigan. All the deer were eating except for one, which was walking on her forefeet. She did this for some time. I told my husband about it and he thought that they might be fighting. But after reading the article we know differently.

In December I observed ten does in the same field. Two larger does were eating ahead of the other ones when four others came running out in circles, back and forth, kicking up their legs. They did this for about ten minutes, then ran into the woods. I know young fawns play like this, but were the deer that I saw playing? I've never seen any do this in December.
C. V., Gaines, Michigan

I can only truthfully answer that I don't know just what it was that the deer were doing.

Despite my many years of observing deer, I have never seen deer walk on their forefeet holding the rear portion of their bodies high. However, I have now received a number of reports from reliable witnesses like you that they

Deer can be very playful, especially in the warm months when food is abundant.

have seen deer do this. It is usually does that are seen doing it. I can only surmise that the deer are playing when they engage in this activity because I can see no practical application for this mode of travel. No one has reported that any of the deer seen doing this were wounded or crippled, thus forcing them to walk in such a manner.

Although hoofed animals do not engage in play as often as do some of the other mammals, notably the predators, they do play far more often than most people suspect. I have witnessed such play many times. I have seen both deer and elk run in water just to see it splash. I've seen both fawns and elk calves play by the hour with a stick, tossing it into the air again and again.

Most of this play that I have witnessed has taken place in spring, summer, and early fall when food was plentiful. Usually the deer and the elk put aside their frivolousness in late October to concentrate all of their efforts on gorging themselves in response to mandatory lipogenesis. If the food in your area was plentiful and the deer were in excellent condition, they may have allowed themselves the luxury of playing even as late as December.

If other readers have ever witnessed deer walking on just their forelegs, I wish they would contact me about it. We all have so much to learn.

I READ WITH great interest your column in *Deer & Deer Hunting* magazine where you mentioned that you had been told by two or three people of seeing white-tailed deer walk on their front legs. I saw just such an incident here in New Hampshire back in late September 1975. It was in the early evening and I was watching four deer feeding out in a large open field. A lone doe came out of the woods and walked toward the other deer, acting very nervous, and walking fairly fast. When she was about 100 feet from the other deer she stopped, jumped around a bit, then suddenly went up on her front feet with her hind legs sticking out behind her like a trick dog. She took three or four steps while in that position and then dropped down to normal. She stood still for a while, looking at the other deer, who were all watching her intently, then shook herself as if she were wet. She then ran over to the other deer and they all ran out of the field.

Have you ever seen deer do this?   *B. B., Londonderry, New Hampshire*

No, I have not seen deer do this, but I now have had six other people tell me about it, with you making number seven. I do not scoff at things people tell me, even if I haven't seen it myself, because I am constantly seeing and learning new things about wildlife. Some biologists try to discredit me because I tell of things I can't prove happened. I have spent thousands upon thousands of hours in the out-of-doors all over the world. I am a very keen observer of everything in nature and I do understand wildlife behavior. When I observe something new I write it down, telling about it so that others will learn from my observations. I hope they will contribute additional information and perhaps follow up with additional research.

One thing you said really got me to thinking. You mentioned how the doe jumped around before she went up on her front feet. I wonder if she was being attacked by a warble fly. When I was a kid back on the family farm our cows would jump around and kick out high with both hind feet and run as fast as they could when the warble flies were laying eggs beneath the skin on their backs. Being more agile and lighter in weight, the deer may have kicked out high and actually walked on its front feet before coming back down. I'm not saying that's what happened, but it is a very plausible explanation. Do any of my readers have anything more to add to this?

I HUNT A lot from three stands around one of my pastures, which is about 600 yards long and 400 yards wide and sort of hourglass shaped. There is quite a bit of traffic out of the woods and across the pasture, especially at either end, mostly does and fawns.

I have noticed that occasionally as she leaves the woods a doe will get disturbed by something and eventually return to the woods the way she came. After that she will not use that exit for several days and no buck will use it during that time. Is she marking it some way that says not to use it right now?

The reason I am sure the doe isn't using it is that we have most of the

When walking, a deer's hind foot track is on top of the track made by the front foot.

breeding does identified — "the big doe," "the old doe," and so forth. They come through our front yard regularly, even during hunting season.

J. M., Colville, Washington

Most deer when they are disturbed, suspicious, or alarmed will stamp their feet. You didn't mention if the disturbed doe that you saw did this. I am willing to bet that she did because you wondered if she was marking the trail somehow since that particular trail would not get used again for several days.

When a deer stamps its feet it marks the ground with an increased amount of scent from its interdigital gland. The scent will definitely alert and warn other deer of the potential danger encountered in that particular spot. That is why a trail is not used for several days.

If the doe did not stamp her feet, I do not know how she could have marked the area.

THE WEEKEND AFTER **New Year 1989** we had about three to four inches of snow. Having some spare time on Saturday, I took a walk in the woods behind my home to look for deer tracks. I am an avid bow hunter and try to spend as much time in the woods studying deer as possible. This was the first snow that we had had that was deep enough to follow tracks and I just wanted to see where the deer were and what they were doing.

The snow had stopped around midnight on Friday night but the deer must have moved early in the evening while it was still snowing because all of the tracks I found had snow in them and nothing was distinct. A pair of the tracks I found were the same size as a deer's tracks, but somehow were different. I found these tracks on the same wood road and going through the same bar-ways as the deer.

I hear that you are working on a book about tracks and I wonder if you can help me. What could those tracks have been?

B. R., Franklin, New Jersey

Without seeing the tracks personally I can't be sure, but from what you have told me I would be willing to bet that the tracks you saw were made by a pair of red foxes. You did say that you saw a pair of tracks. January is the breeding season for the red fox and they begin to pair up in December. From that time until the female gives birth to her pups in April the male and female foxes are inseparable. Following their tracks in the snow is most interesting because the tracks are found side by side, then they split apart as the foxes investigate something, then they come back together. Many times, especially if the snow is deeper, the second fox walks precisely in the tracks made by the first fox. At such a time you would swear that you were following the tracks of a single fox. Just when you have convinced yourself that there is only one fox, the tracks split apart as they go around opposite sides of a brushy area as the fox hunt for food.

The red fox's foot makes about the same size track as a deer's. If the tracks were fresh, you would have had no trouble seeing either the toe marks of the fox or the hoof prints of the deer. With drifted snow the holes poked in the snow by either animal would be about the same size. However, the normal trotting stride of the red fox is about fourteen inches while that of a walking deer is seventeen to eighteen inches. The fox's tracks will be closer together than those of the deer. In addition, deer will always have drag marks in front of their tracks whenever there is over one-half inch of snow. In just three to four inches of snow there will be no drag marks in front of the fox's tracks because

Deer always leave drag marks in front of their tracks when there is more than a half inch of snow.

they pick their feet up high enough to prevent their dragging in the snow. You can always tell which way the deer are going because the drag marks are always in front of their hoof tracks. If the snow is drifted, as in this case, it is sometimes difficult to tell which way a fox is going because there are no drag marks. A really close examination of the tracks should show a slight angled depression on the rear of the fox's track, made as it put its foot forward before putting its weight on it.

I love to track wildlife in snow. It's like reading the latest newspaper. It tells you what went where, when, why, and with what. It's all written out for you if you can read sign.

The mark of cloven hooves is obvious here. These tracks were made by black-tailed deer.

MY QUESTION INVOLVES **an incident I had a few years back. It was mid-October during the 1987 bow-hunting season, and I was heading out to my stand in the afternoon and was surprised to see a doe already feeding in the alfalfa field that I was going to hunt over. I was completely camouflaged but I wasn't wearing any scent, so I decided to have a little fun. I was on one side of a pasture connecting to the field so I didn't have much cover. I started crawling toward the doe but she noticed me almost immediately. The wind was at my back and I figured that it wouldn't be long before she would be bounding into the woods, but, to my surprise, she started coming toward me, bobbing her head, and never taking her eyes off me. Then I tried to imitate her, bobbing my head and standing on my hands and knees. She kept coming! I had her to within ten yards before she walked off, seemingly confused. She was a young doe. Was this a "dumb" deer or was there something that I did that I was unaware of?** *N. J., Hatley, Wisconsin*

Deer are extremely curious. Although you say the wind was at your back, it is very evident that that doe did not get your scent. If she had, she would have dashed off as you had expected her to do. Somehow the wind currents veered or eddied or she would not have been curious any longer; she would have known what you were.

The fact that you were dressed in camouflage broke up your outline so she could not identify what she was seeing, but, as you say, she saw you instantly when you moved. The fact that you were on your hands and knees made you much smaller than she was, so that made you much less of a threat.

Caribou are famous for their head-bobbing communication. The cows urge their calves on by head-bobbing and bulls use it to challenge one another. It is a very important part of their language, meaning different things under different circumstances and instances. Many times I have gotten much closer to caribou by bending forward at the waist, extending my arms out, and bobbing up and down as I slowly approached. And they have let me get quite close.

What is not so well known is that head-bobbing also has importance in white-tailed deer communication. Because a fawn is so much smaller than the doe, she approaches the fawn with her head down, frequently bobbing it up and down. Deer that detect danger will head-bob and this bobbing transmits a danger implication to other deer. In this same danger situation deer will frequently move their heads from one side to the other, almost as if they were trying to get two different angles of vision to give them a better triangular "fix" in order to determine distance.

Curiosity is a sign of intelligence. Your doe was not a "dumb" deer; she was just trying to figure out an answer to a puzzle she couldn't solve.

We have a great deal to learn about deer and one of the greatest areas is that of communication. With our use of rattling antlers, scents, and grunt calls we now have a good beginning, but we still have a long way to go.

I HAVE READ many times that white-tailed deer will not cross a hunter's track. I know that I have had deer follow my tracks because I have seen their tracks in the snow on top of mine. Do you feel that deer will readily cross a human's track or that they turn back?
M. S., New York, New York

There is no hard-and-fast answer to this question because circumstances alter situations. In general, a deer is not afraid of a human's track.

In my home area of northwestern New Jersey a deer cannot move without crossing tracks of humans. I believe all deer become aware of a human's track as soon as they come to it. Their reaction to the track depends on the pressure that has been put on the deer. If the deer are in a protected area where they are not exposed to danger, they couldn't care less. During the hunting season the deer are much more aware of the potential danger but they would cross a human's track in my area because they are practically forced to do so.

In a wilderness area where people are seldom encountered the deer may shy away from the track or be drawn to it out of curiosity. A wise old buck who has been driven up on the more remote ridges by hunting pressure probably would do everything within his ability to get away from any human scent.

WHY WOULD A deer walk with the wind at its tail? Many people would swear it to be wrong, including me, if I hadn't sighted a deer doing just that. While sitting on a birch deadfall after completing a brief still hunt, I heard a branch snap. I thought nothing of it at the time because the sound was coming from the north and so was the wind. About two minutes later I slowly turned and saw a steady black dot bouncing along. Much to my amazement it was the nose of a deer walking with the wind. It then turned off the logging road and walked crosswind through the woods. One short prayer and a twenty-gauge slug equaled my first buck deer.

Could the reason be that a deer while walking with the wind can

LEN RUE, JR.

Walking into the wind allows a deer to focus its senses—smell, sight, and hearing—on what is in front of it.

both see and hear anything in front of it and smell what is behind it instead of using all its senses for what is in front of it only?

E. C., Greendale, Wisconsin

Deer usually walk into the wind because they can then smell, hear, and see anything in front of them. Also, as they walk, they are getting farther from anything pursuing or sneaking up on them. You are also right in assuming that a buck walking with the wind can smell anything behind him and, at the same time, hear and see anything in front of him. Because the sense of smell is the deer's keenest sense, in time of danger, such as hunting pressure, the buck will walk into the wind rather than with it when it is possible.

However, 50 percent, or at least 25 percent, of the time a buck will be walking with the wind behind him under normal circumstances. Almost every area has a prevailing wind direction and in this country it usually comes from the west in varying angles. Winds can change anywhere and they can blow from any direction, but our prevailing wind is westerly.

If deer did not walk with the wind 50 percent of the time, or at the very least 25 percent of the time, they would never get back to where they started. If deer did not walk with the wind behind them, the bulk of them would end up on the east coast. Perhaps that's why New Jersey hunters are allowed so many deer per season.

I N REFERENCE TO **your book** *The World of the White-Tailed Deer,* **one of the things that I would like to ask you is how did you find so many deer at one time? In the photograph on page 92 there are seventy deer feeding in the field. I think that is amazing! Another amazing photograph is on page 70 where the two males are fighting for the female.** *M. T., Castleton, New York*

Folks who know of my work with deer are often surprised when they find out that I live in New Jersey. Actually, the area that I live in has one of the highest deer-per-square-mile populations in the country. We really do have more deer than we have food to feed them over the winter. That is the main reason why New Jersey has such liberal deer hunting seasons. Our hunters, with the proper licenses and in the proper seasons, are able to take twenty-one deer per year. I don't know of any hunter who takes even half that number, but he has the opportunity to try.

There really is no secret to finding concentrations of deer, particularly in the winter. You can go to deer yards where the deer go—in hollows, cedar thickets, or swamps where they will be out of the wind. Or you can go to some area where food is available and where there is no wind. Deer can stand extreme cold; they just can't stand cold driven by the wind.

Several years ago I photographed an even larger concentration of deer than that in the photo you mentioned. In a field just twelve miles from my home I counted 110 deer. However, the field was a large one and the deer were widely scattered across it. If I had used a wide-angle lens, I could have gotten all the deer in the photo but they would have been just small black specks. By using a telephoto lens I got only thirty deer in each photograph, but the deer do show up well.

The deer were feeding on the old cabbage stalks and leaves that were left

A large, but widely spread out, group of deer feeding.

after the heads of cabbage had been harvested. Just think of the problem that farmer must have had the following spring when he had to set out the new cabbage seedlings. Too many deer can be a problem, too.

YOU SAY THAT white-tailed deer don't migrate, yet just a few miles west of Cortland, New York, in September 1985 I saw an estimated 300 deer, three or four abreast in a long line, come off a hill, cross the road, go down a gully, up the other side, cross a field, and go into the woods beyond. I'm not the only one who saw the deer because I was the fourth car in a line that had stopped to let the deer cross the road and to watch. Unfortunately, none of us had a camera. Was this a migration?
                                                        L. M., Cortland, New York

It sounds like a migration. I have never seen 300 whitetails together at any time. Mule deer, which do migrate, may travel in numbers that high. There is some shifting of whitetails from summer range to winter range in northern Michigan and Wisconsin, but the distance is only twenty to thirty miles and it is done by family groups. I have not seen, nor have I even read of, that many whitetails moving as you have described it. Lacking a camera, it's too bad that you didn't get the names and addresses of all the witnesses in order to substantiate and verify your sighting.

Part Three

Habitat and Management

A T THE TIME of the coming of the white man to the North American continent, what area did the white-tailed deer inhabit?

J. G., Livonia, Michigan

According to archaeological records the white-tailed deer inhabited the entire area east of the Mississippi River and west of it to the Rocky Mountains for thousands upon thousands of years. It is generally conceded that the Indians have been on this continent for at least eighteen thousand years. The excavation of the mound-builders of Ohio and other Indian prehistoric sites all show the remnants of white-tailed deer being used as food and clothing. The deer's antlers were often used by the Indians on their headgear for religious cere-

Several deer grazing in the southwestern United States. White-tailed deer are plentiful in most areas east of the Rocky Mountains.

monies and were practically accorded deity status.

The deer were not as numerous then as they are now because the deer did not thrive in mature forests. However, wherever lightning or the Indians had burned clearings in the forest – so vegetation could be started – the deer multiplied. In fact, the Indians were the first game managers because they had learned to open up the primal forest by fire in order to establish larger deer herds.

I AM TWENTY-FIVE years old and have not missed a deer season since I was twelve. I consider myself a knowledgeable deer hunter from personal experience and reading every type of whitetail literature I can get my hands on, but I now have a problem. My father and I own two pieces of property in northern Wisconsin, one of which (near Eagle River) we have hunted almost exclusively since 1970. This property is small and we have been hunting on neighboring property, which is increasingly becoming posted. We are slowly beginning to hunt on our other property, where we have much more land to hunt on.

Our problem is this: We are finding less and less deer sign on our land and we would very much like to hunt it. In the summer of 1985 we built a tree stand in a seemingly perfect hunting area, on top of a ridge with good visibility. When deer season arrived we decided to try it for one day, but found very little sign. We would like to attract more deer to this area but are not sure how to do it, knowing that deer will change their habits.

We considered some options: planting apple trees, clover, or certain vegetables; providing salt licks; even putting out piles of potatoes. The problem with apples is the time it takes for the trees to mature. The problem with clover or vegetables is that by deer season they would be snow covered. Deer like salt, but not during the gun season. And, finally, hunting near potato piles, although a common practice in our area, might be illegal.

To add to our problem, our time to spend at this area is limited because we actually live in a Milwaukee suburb and cannot spend a lot of time at the area at one time. What can we do to bring the deer back to our property, which we really wish to hunt on?

G. B., Brookfield, Wisconsin

You have two problems—problems that are becoming many other hunters' problems, too. Number one is that increasingly more land is being closed to hunting by being posted. This problem can only accelerate in the very near future as our human population continues to grow. This means that larger tracts of land are being broken into smaller blocks that are owned by more people, many of whom either want to hunt the land themselves or who will just close it to all hunting.

The second problem is that you are experiencing a declining deer population despite the fact that the nation as a whole is experiencing a steady increase. Your declining deer population can be the result of either the area being overhunted or poached, or your land growing back into a mature forest. Not being able to see the situation for myself, I suspect it is probably the latter.

You did not tell me how many acres you had or what the topography of the land is, except to say that you put your stand on the top of a ridge in what should have been a good spot for deer. You did not say if it was a good spot for deer.

I find this a very common fault with many hunters: they put their stands in spots that to them look like good deer country. Instead, they should do extensive preseason scouting and put their stands where trails, rubs, scrapes, or signs of feeding activity pinpoint where the deer actually are. You didn't say whether you saw good sign when you first put up your stand. If you did, then you have reason to be surprised that there was very little sign when hunting season started. Now you have to discover why the deer changed their pattern of activity. My guess is that the deer were not there in the first place because of a lack of food in the area.

In the August 1987 issue of *Deer & Deer Hunting* magazine I answered a letter similar to yours in my column. What I wrote about land management there also applies to your situation. If after you read that you still have questions, please don't hesitate to write again.

WE HAVE ABOUT **800 acres of mixed woodland and farmland here in eastern Virginia and our deer herd is growing. We harvest bmth bucks and does and there is lots of good deer food. Our problem is that we have more does than we do bucks and would like to have it the other way around. What can we do to produce more bucks than does?** *J. C., Richmond, Virginia*

If you want to have more bucks than does, the simplest solution is to shoot more does than bucks. But that's not what you asked. You want to know how you can "produce" more bucks than you do does. However, I'm not sure that you really want that condition to exist.

You claim that your deer herd is growing and that you have lots of deer food on your property. That can only mean that your herd is still expanding and that you have not yet reached, or exceeded, the carrying capacity of your land.

It has been proven that where the does are well nourished, as they would be on your land, they give birth to a higher number of doe fawns than they do bucks. Having more doe fawns allows for more breeding stock and thus allows the herd's population to increase.

Conversely, when the land's carrying capacity has been reached, and particularly where it has been exceeded, the ratio shifts to a much higher percentage of buck fawns being born. This in turn reduces the overall deer population because there is less breeding stock, thus allowing the vegetation to recover. Many types of birds and animals are cyclic, having periods of peak population

LEN RUE, JR.

When the number of deer is less than the carrying capacity of the land, the deer will be much better nourished.

and population crashes, then gradual, timed recoveries. Deer are not cyclic; their population is governed by the amount of food available to them.

As I said, I'm not sure that you really want to produce more bucks because it would mean that both your deer herd and its habitat were deteriorating rapidly. Under those conditions your herd would be producing more bucks per doe, but the overall number of bucks produced would be lower because there would be less does producing fawns.

At the present time you are enjoying about the best your herd can produce. My only recommendation is that you continue to harvest both bucks and does as you have been doing and perhaps take a few more does than you have been in order to keep your herd at the peak of its breeding potential, but below the carrying capacity of the land. If you harvest both the bucks and the does, you should be able to produce more quality bucks because more food will be available to the deer that are left after the hunting season.

You have an ideal situation.

A mineral block helps deer
get the nutrients they need.

I BELONG TO a hunting club that owns several hundred acres of land with most of our forest being mature trees. Will we get bigger deer if we try to manage the land?
C. F., Albany, New York

Yes. The body size of the deer and their antlers can definitely be increased by good land management.

Without seeing your club land I can only give generalizations. One of the easiest things to do is to make sure that your deer herd has access to all of the minerals that it needs. I would suggest that you mix "Deer Lix" with salt as recommended and place it at different sites around your property near deer trails.

If you have some level land that could be cleared, you could plant the land to crops such as alfalfa, clover, corn, rye, or buckwheat.

Thinning a forest does not really help the deer because not enough sunlight reaches the forest floor. If not on a steep hillside, I would recommend clear-cutting areas of about ten acres. Cut the trees in the fall, allow the deer to

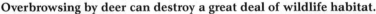

Overbrowsing by deer can destroy a great deal of wildlife habitat.

browse the tops over the winter, and burn the leftover brush in the spring to return the minerals to the soil. The logs can be used for lumber and the branches and lesser trees can be used for firewood. Fertilize the soil well and allow for natural regeneration of the forest. In three to four years after clearing the land you will have a deer's idea of paradise as the new brush grows profusely, and you will see a very definite increase in both your deer's body size and in the antler development.

In two to three years after the initial clearing, cut off another ten acres and keep repeating this pattern. You will get maximum growth and profit from your forest and also from your deer.

You might want to plant copses of evergreens of about one acre or so to provide shelter for the deer in cold weather. You might want to leave some of the best mature oaks uncut to provide mast in the fall. Do not clear-cut steep hillsides because it may cause erosion.

When you cut the trees for firewood, but not those for timber, cut the stumps four feet above the ground. I don't know why, but the extra height to the stump promotes far more sprouting than a low-cut stump. The year after the sprouts have come up you can go back and cut the stump close to the ground. You get all of the wood and produce excellent deer food in the process.

IS IT IMPORTANT **to have evergreens on winter deer range and how big an area would it have to be?** *T. Q., Buffalo, New York*

Evergreens are a very important part of winter deer range in your area and all other northern states. The evergreens have to be in stands, or blocks, to be effective. Single trees help, but to be really useful there has to be a good-sized area of at least one acre or so of continuous evergreens with most of them being over ten inches in diameter.

Evergreens of that size have branches strong enough to hold up a good snow load. The depth of snow below a stand of evergreens is usually only one-half to one-third the depth of snow that actually falls. The trees hold the rest of the snow aloft. This means that the deer are much more able to move around searching for food.

On the other hand, an extensive stand of hundreds of acres of evergreens is of little use to the deer because if the trees are mature they will prevent up to 90 percent of the sunshine from getting to the forest floor. Without that sunlight no vegetation can grow beneath the evergreens. So, although the deer may be able to move about more easily, there is nothing for them to feed on by moving about.

The ideal situation is when there are blocks of conifers interspersed with blocks of new-growth hardwoods. The deer can be sheltered in the evergreens but can search for food among the hardwoods.

Another important aspect of the conifer stands is that their cover prevents radiant heat loss from the deer and provides good protection against the wind. Deer can easily withstand periods of extreme cold because of the insulative qualities of their coats, but they cannot withstand cold combined with strong winds because the wind destroys the effectiveness of their coats. During periods of extreme cold a deer that is protected from the wind expends less calories than a deer that is not protected. Under these circumstances the protection from the wind is of greater importance than is the mobility to gather food. It is not likely that the deer that is moving around will take in as many calories of food as it would be losing through exposure to the wind.

A stand of young evergreens will break up the wind but cannot support the snow load because their branches bend down under the weight. An advantage of having the branches bend, however, is that it often brings the tips that could not otherwise be used for food down within reach of the deer.

I WAS DEER **hunting in Pennsylvania one extremely frosty morning. We had had two days of rain and the frozen leaves made a noise like glass breaking every time I put my foot down. In going to my stand I had to pass through a rather extensive area of mature white pines and hemlocks. It was like entering a different world; I could walk on the leaves that had blown under those trees without making a sound as they were just wet, not frozen. Why hadn't the leaves and needles frozen under those evergreen trees?** *C. W., State College, Pennsylvania*

All trees produce a microclimate, with evergreen trees changing the temperature as much as eight to ten degrees.

Hardwoods, the deciduous trees, break up some of the force of the wind, reducing the chill factor a bit. All trees give off an infinitesimal amount of heat, even during cold winter nights. During the winter days they absorb heat, melting the snow around them, with the darker trees absorbing and giving off the greater amount.

You have discovered why it is so important in the northern half of the United States to have stands of evergreens scattered throughout the deer's winter range. Evergreens, being dark, absorb more of the sun's rays during the daytime and their branches slow down the heat loss at night. The evergreens present a much more effective wind barrier than do the deciduous trees. During snowstorms the branches of the evergreens often hold most or all of the snowfall aloft. Many times in dense stands of conifers almost no snow reaches the ground, and unless a strong wind dislodges the snow it may melt from the branches keeping the ground beneath snow-free. The dark forest duff (the dropped needles) absorbs the sunlight instead of its being reflected by the snow, raising the temperature substantially. To the deer on a starvation diet the difference of six, eight, or ten degrees in temperature can often mean the difference between survival and death. The slightly higher temperatures beneath the evergreens means that the deer will have to expend fewer calories to keep their body temperature normal.

Yes, evergreens are often critical to the deer's survival. If you don't have any on the land you hunt, plant them. Be sure to plant them in blocks.

WE HAVE A **hunting camp in northwestern Pennsylvania that is about 160 acres of mostly woodland that adjoins some state game land. Lately the deer seem to be getting smaller, with smaller-sized antlers. We do see quite a few deer in the area. We have no fields on our club, but would like to do something besides supplemental feeding of the deer to see if we can get bigger, better deer. Do you have any suggestions?** *T. O., Philadelphia, Pennsylvania*

If you have no fields and don't want to do supplemental feeding, which is costly, you have only two options open to you. Because you have only 160 acres, or one-fourth of a square mile, a lot of what you do will be of little benefit because your deer will be ranging over an area as much as four to eight times larger than your property. However, every little bit helps and I would advise you to try to implement one or both of the options open to you.

Because you have a wooded area I would suggest you contact your state forester for help in implementing forest management practices with the main thrust of your program being to benefit the deer.

If it is at all possible, I would suggest that you clear-cut several five-acre blocks of woodland, leaving only the mature oaks standing for their mast production. If you apply some fertilizer to the soil and then just allow the area to grow up in brush, you will have a good start on managing your land for deer. If there are no evergreen areas on your land, I would suggest you plant some

The clear-cut swaths necessary for power lines create good edge and browse for deer.

200-by-200-foot blocks of evergreen seedlings to give the deer protection against the weather. Be sure to also put out mineral blocks for the deer.

If your deer and their antlers are getting smaller, then you have more deer than your land and the state game lands will support. Your second option is to reduce the number of deer that are on your land. This is hard medicine because everyone likes to see lots of deer. But lots of deer consume lots of food and unless your herd is reduced your game management plans are doomed before you start. If your club cannot legally kill enough deer to effect this reduction, invite other hunters to help out.

Research done in Pennsylvania has shown that for forested areas such as yours thirteen to fourteen deer to the square mile is about optimum. When the deer population increases beyond that number it prohibits regular forest regeneration and reduces forage diversity. The deer will consume all of their favorite, or the more palatable, food plants and trees, allowing the area to grow up with the least desirable species, thus making the area even more inhospitable to the deer.

You really should seek to drastically reduce the number of deer in your area prior to starting your management practices, or at least do them simultaneously. In actuality you will have to remove almost all of the deer in your area because as you lessen the deer pressure on your land it will pull in additional deer from the surrounding areas. After the herd has been reduced and the brush is growing back on the cut-over areas the deer will increase both in numbers and in size.

I LIVE IN **Lenawee County in southern Michigan. I am an avid bow hunter. The past few years Michigan has offered two deer tags, and anyone who sends for a doe tag gets one. This year they offered a bonus deer tag, which allows us to shoot five deer. I've noticed over the past three years the deer herd in Lenawee County has slowly decreased. In the thirty-nine days I hunted this past bow season I averaged one deer sighting every four days. The state says that we have fifteen to twenty deer per square mile. That rating is eight to ten deer too high, yet they keep killing them off. I guess they'll do anything to make a dollar. Why not make a dollar by saving our doe population? What can I do as a lone person to help bring the deer population back?**

C. H., Lenawee County, Michigan

I really don't know what the situation is in Lenawee County, Michigan. It may be that the state is deliberately trying to lower the overall deer-herd population in that area to lessen crop damage, shrubbery damage, or deer-car accidents. That is precisely what my own state of New Jersey is trying to do—because they have to. We simply do not have enough natural food, such as browse, to feed the number of deer we have through a hard winter. In any area we average about thirty to thirty-five deer per square mile and hundreds of deer are killed by cars each year in a ten- to fifteen-mile radius of my home. Our deer herd is estimated to be between 150,000 and 165,000 and, with all of the seasons, tags, and permits, a hunter is allowed twenty-one deer. Our deer herd will have to decline if for no other reason than the rapid urbanization of our rural areas.

If that is not your state's intent and reason, then you have a different set of problems. Is your habitat declining? Is your area also being built up? Are the deer actually being overhunted?

If the answer is yes to the first two questions, then that is the core of your problem. If the answer to the first two questions is no, then I will go along with your observation that the deer are being overhunted. Anyone who is as interested in the deer situation as you are, and spends as much time afield as you have, just has to be knowledgeable about the deer and their population.

If the herd is declining due to overhunting, you, as an individual, can do a number of things. You can restrict the number of deer you personally take, or you can shoot bucks only. Ducks Unlimited has asked their members to do just that—shoot less and take only males in an effort to help the duck population recover from the devastation caused by recent droughts. You can appeal to your game department to change the law; you can petition your local legislators to speak to the game department on your behalf. You can write letters to the editors of all the local papers expressing your viewpoint and opinion in this matter.

You really can do much more as a group than as an individual. Speak out at all the local gun hunting clubs in your area and make this a group effort. You can try to enlist the United Hunting Clubs of Michigan, a very powerful lobbying group, to help get the situation corrected. There are many things that you can do and you, as an individual, can be the spark plug that gets the entire situation fired up.

Ascertain the purpose, get the facts, then go to it.

I READ YOUR **article in the June 1990 issue of** *Deer & Deer Hunting* **and was shocked to read that in New Jersey a person can possibly get twenty-one deer in one season. What is the reason for so many deer per hunter for one hunting season? I can't understand how any state could have a limit that high.** *M. W., Eastlake, Ohio*

I believe that New Jersey has one of the best deer-management programs in the country. The state is divided up into game-management areas and each area is managed accordingly. Each area is censused and the special seasons and doe limits are set on that basis with heavier harvesting being done where needed and held back if such action is warranted.

New Jersey has a very high human population, with about 1,000 people per square mile. It also has a high deer population, estimated at 157,000. New Jersey has 7,521 square miles of land and that comes to 20.8 deer to the square mile. Twenty deer to the square mile is usually considered the optimum number in good habitat. However, none of these figures takes into account that so many square miles of land in New Jersey have no deer habitat at all, that a great part of the state is unending megalopolis. That pushes the deer herd onto the land that is still available. Many areas of the state have as many as fifty deer to the square mile and we do not have enough natural food to feed them. Destruction of farm crops is high, as is the destruction of plantings and shrubbery.

We also have a high toll of highway kills. The New Jersey deer herd must be controlled, and the most efficient and economical way to do it is to have the herd curtailed by legalized sport hunting.

Because of the heavy hunting pressure in New Jersey about 85 percent of all of our bucks are killed when they are just one and one-half years old. New Jersey doesn't have a single buck in the Boone and Crockett record book. New Jersey has produced some large deer and some trophy bucks; in fact, there are three large enough to be listed in the Boone and Crockett book. I don't know why they are not. They are listed in the New Jersey trophy book.

New Jersey does offer fantastic deer hunting. Hunters in New Jersey have the potential of spending 101 days deer hunting in six special seasons with a possible bag limit of twenty-one deer with all the necessary permits. New Jersey is not only producing deer, it is producing an almost unequaled opportunity to hunt them.

The 1988/89 deer harvest was a total of 45,900 deer, with 22,344 of them being bucks. Bow hunters took 9,816 deer. I don't know of anyone who has taken twenty deer in one season although I do know of a family of three that took fourteen.

If you want to take a lot of deer, you might try South Carolina where most counties have no daily or seasonal bag limit and the season extends from the middle of August to the first of January. Or you might try Alabama where the bow-hunting limit is one deer of either sex per day from October 14 through January 31 for a total of 123 days, or deer, however you want to count it.

The "good old days" of deer hunting are today.

I CAUGHT THE **tail end of a radio talk show interview with a deer biologist from Michigan. They talked about the cultural carrying capacity of the land. I attended your white-tailed deer seminar in Wausau and you explained the carrying capacity of the land for deer but you did not mention the cultural carrying capacity. What is it all about?** *E. W., Wausau, Wisconsin*

The carrying capacity of any given area for deer is when the deer herd has sufficient food in its habitat to survive the winter. The cultural carrying capacity is a new term coined by a Connecticut deer biologist a few years ago. It defines the actual number of deer that is desired, or that will be tolerated, by the people who own the land that the deer live on.

About twenty years ago I was contacted by a group that called itself the Deer Protective Association. They gave me no hint as to their activities, but they asked me to put on one of my white-tailed deer seminars. Judging from their name I assumed that these people really loved deer and wanted information on how best to manage their lands in order to increase the deer-herd population by increasing the actual carrying capacity of the land.

We were both shocked after we met and I began to talk. They didn't want to know how to increase the number of deer on their property; they wanted to know how to get rid of all the deer they had. The club was composed of very wealthy people who had large estates and land holdings in the Mendham-Bernardsville area of New Jersey. Since they allowed no hunting on their lands, the deer herd had multiplied astronomically and was wreaking havoc on their ornamental shrubbery.

When I understood their problem, and I do understand it—a single deer can consume all the tips off three sixty-dollar yew shrubs in a single night—I suggested a number of ways that they could combat their problems. No, they wouldn't open their lands to hunting; they didn't want anybody walking on their properties and shooting everything in sight. No, they didn't want any bow hunters either. I named some sprays that could be put on their shrubs, but they complained about the odor of some that they had already tried. And no fences, either, thank you; they were unsightly.

They had too many deer, but in actuality they didn't want any deer at all. The carrying capacity of their land was exceeded, but the cultural carrying capacity of their land was zero.

Although I didn't agree with them, I realized that their complaint was legitimate and they had every right to voice their opinion. Game managers in the future will have to take into consideration the wishes of such people; they do own the land on which the state's deer live. However, the game managers do not have to correct the situation as long as the lands these people own are closed to even limited hunting. Regulated sport hunting is still the best game management tool we have.

Just recently, 170 deer were counted on my neighbor's farm. He likes deer and often leaves corn standing to help them through the winter. However, his alfalfa crops are being devastated and the deer population will have to be reduced.

Farmers and orchardists want the deer controlled. Insurance companies paying for deer damage to vehicles would like to see them eliminated. Nature lovers like to see deer; foresters do, too, unless the deer are preventing the regeneration of new forest growth.

All of these people have legitimate demands and requirements. It is a very complex problem and there are no easy answers, but all of their diverse requirements will have to be taken into consideration in all future planning for the management of the deer-herd population. That is what cultural carrying capacity is all about.

WE HAVE MANY **dense, almost unhuntable swamp tracts up here in our area. Do you think that by getting back into them I could take a trophy buck?** *C. W., Hayward, Wisconsin*

It probably would not be worth the time or effort. While it is true that there are many inaccessible swamps, forests, and mountainous regions throughout the country where the deer hunting pressure is light, that doesn't mean that these areas are going to produce trophy bucks. It is true that a number of the deer in such areas may get old enough to become trophy bucks because they are not hunted heavily, but it is equally true that in extensive forest areas, tamarack swamps, and so forth, there is little good deer food. Such areas are inaccessible because there are no roads going into them. It means that the vegetation is probably climax forest growth and that it always has been. Climax forest growth usually shades out all emerging vegetation and unless a fire has been set by lightning there is no plant succession growth. So although the deer may get old enough to get to be trophy bucks, they are not likely to have the abundance of nutritious food that it takes to develop the antlers on trophy bucks.

In the dense tamarack swamps in your area of northwestern Wisconsin it is not likely that you could even see the deer. In one experiment, in a one-square-mile enclosure in northern Michigan, it took six hunters a combined 124 hours of hunting to see just one of the seven bucks that were in the enclosure. I don't think it's worth your time to go back into those deep swamps.

WHILE HUNTING FOR **mule deer in Colorado I was bunked in with a hunter from Washington State who was a forester. We got to talking about white-tailed deer and I told him about how destructive the deer are to the vegetation in my area. Here in Westches-**

ter County the deer are actually devastating the shrubbery around all of our houses. The deer particularly like Japanese yew and eat them right down to the trunks.

I have tried tying bags of human hair on the shrubbery, but I have had only limited success with it. When the weather got extremely cold the deer paid no attention to the hair and ate my shrubs anyway. They must have been desperate. The forester said that the big timber companies out West were planting selenium tablets with each Douglas fir seedling and that the deer wouldn't touch them.

Have you ever heard of this and do you think it would work here in the East? *W. B., White Plains, New York*

Tying bags of human hair on shrubbery is usually an effective deer repellent. It didn't work during the extremely cold weather because extreme cold tends to crystallize the molecules of scent, making any scent much harder to detect. The deer just didn't smell the hair during that period.

Yes, I have heard of planting selenium tablets with seedlings. Selenium is found naturally in many of the soils in the western states. Livestock will usually eat the vegetation grown on selenium-rich soils, but most of the deer, antelope, and elk will not. When the selenium in the soil is absorbed by the plants' roots the plants give off a very strong garlic odor through their leaves and needles. Evidently this makes the plants repugnant to the wild animals. Researchers have found that time-released selenium pills provide up to three years' protection for the firs from the deer.

I don't know if selenium would work with other plants, but I don't know why it wouldn't. I suggest that you try putting some time-released selenium tablets in the soil around the roots of your shrubbery to see if it works. The tablets cost very little. I would be cautious about using it in a vegetable garden as a deterrent for deer, however, because excessive amounts can cause selenium poisoning.

I AM NOT a hunter, although my husband is. I don't have any real feelings about hunting one way or the other. If hunting keeps him happy, then let him hunt. After all, having a happy husband is much more important to me than the issue of hunting. He has tried to interest me in hunting, and I do enjoy driving out in the country to see the deer while he does his "scouting," as he calls it. I don't quite see how he can enjoy hunting the deer after getting so much enjoyment out of

The browse line shows the highest point on trees and branches that the deer can reach.

just looking at them. He keeps claiming that if the deer were not hunted, their population would grow so big that they would destroy their habitat. Why would deer deliberately destroy their own habitat and how would they do it? *Mrs. H. B., Youngstown, Ohio*

Deer don't intend to destroy their habitat, but they do through sheer increases in their population. Just think of the amount of development that has occurred in just the past ten or twenty years. I am sure you have seen many rural areas developed into urban centers. More people means more consumption; and the greater the consumption, the greater the pollution, garbage, and toxic waste. We will never be able to control anything in this world if we don't control our human population. That, basically, is what hunting is all about – control.

A deer herd with an adequate food supply will have an annual recruitment rate of about 40 percent per year. Eventually, and it is usually in four years, the herd will increase in population until it about equals the annual vegetative growth rate. From then on it is all downhill for the habitat. The herd will continue to increase in population for another two to three years at the most, then will plateau and begin a gradual decline as the food shortages begin to affect the deer in many ways.

On good food about 40 to 60 percent of the spring-born doe fawns will breed in the fall. Usually a doe has a single fawn the first time she gives birth and then twins are the norm thereafter. On exceptionally nutritious food the doe may actually produce triplets.

Although deer can ordinarily feed on 500 to 600 different types of vegetation, they are selective feeders, having food preferences just as we do. When a deer population has reached its peak it will, in a very short period of time, consume all of its preferred foods and much of its secondary choices.

A white-tailed buck creating the browse line.

When a deer population exceeds its food supply it is forced to feed on whatever is available that it can eat. By this time both the preferred and secondary choices of food have been destroyed and will be prevented from coming back as they will be eaten as fast as they grow back. Because of this the deer have the ability to completely change the vegetation that grows in the area, since only rejected vegetation can survive. Deer can absolutely prevent forest regeneration.

This is not accomplished without its taking a toll on the deer. First of all, the deer cannot get enough nutritious food. Then, when they cannot get adequate food the spring-born doe fawns do not breed because they have not developed enough physically to be able to do so. The adult does are not able to bear twins and, in extreme cases, they will not have any young at all. Even if they each have a single fawn, the does' milk supply will be sharply curtailed and the mortality potential of the fawns will be exceedingly high. The fawns that are born and nursed will be smaller in size than is normal when winter comes and they will probably perish.

On a reduced food intake over an extended period of time – and it may take ten to twenty years for a denuded habitat to begin to come back – the general physical size of the deer will be smaller, lighter in weight, and the bucks' antlers will be much smaller than they ought to be. The herd will continue to deteriorate and to decline in population until it is low enough for the vegetation to begin to come back. After the vegetation starts to come back – and many species of plants never will – the deer herd will start to increase. Deer do not have definite yearly cycles like such animals as the ruffed grouse, the various mice and lemmings, or the gray squirrel. They are on a "boom-and-bust" cycle that is tied to vegetative growth. We hunt deer to control their numbers in order to prevent the destruction of the habitat and the deterioration of the deer.

Deer are also very destructive to the habitat in more subtle ways. Prior to and during the rutting season bucks are very busy advertising their presence by making scrapes and rubs. A buck may make a dozen rubs per day for a period of about three to four months. Sometimes he rubs a sapling that has been rubbed before, but most of the time he makes a brand-new rub. If he rubs the sapling on just one side, it will live, although the debarked area will probably cause the tree to rot as it grows larger. If the buck rubs the tree all the way around, effectively girdling the tree, it will die because the fibrovascular bundles, the tree's water pipes, will have been cut. Thus, a single buck has the potential of killing up to a thousand saplings each fall. And although these saplings will be spread out over a ten-to-twelve-square-mile area, that's still a lot of trees. And there are many bucks doing it.

LEN RUE, JR.

The author with a twelve-inch buck rub. Just one buck making several such rubs over a three- or four-month period adds up to a lot of tree destruction.

Deer can also cause considerable erosion, their sharp hoofs tearing up the protective turf. It is well known that wildlife will walk up a hill by the easiest gradient. However, on a really steep hill they have to go up on a steep grade. Where a number of deer use the same trail the vegetation is soon killed and the topsoil chopped up. Without the vegetation's roots to hold the topsoil the rains soon cause the trail to erode. According to the number of deer, the amount of rain, and the steepness of the gradient, the trail soon becomes a gully down which the water cascades. I have seen steep hillsides literally torn apart by deer's hoofs.

THERE HAS BEEN a great upsurge reported in the number of bucks that are killed on the highways during rutting season. Although the number of both sexes killed increases during this period, the kill is primarily of bucks. Do you have any idea how much more a buck is at risk of being killed on the highway during the rut than at other times of the year?   *O. C., Erie, Pennsylvania*

ACCORDING TO YOUR book *The Deer of North America,* May and November are the months in which most deer are killed on the highways by automobiles. That may be true, but in driving along the back roads of our area I have been seeing more deer than usual out in the road in the latter part of September. Why?

L. P., Mt. Cresco, Pennsylvania

This question has intrigued me for some time. Although the figures that I'm about to give are not cast in concrete, I do hope they will stimulate some game department or group of biologists to conduct controlled experiments. My work is based solely on many years of observations and intuitive deductions.

November has the greatest number of fatalities among deer over most of the United States because that is the peak of the rutting season and all of the deer, both bucks and does, are moving more than at any other time of the year. The bucks have expanded their home ranges from one to two square miles to ten to twelve square miles in their search for receptive does. That means they are crossing not only more roads but also unfamiliar roads. And, since it is the rutting season, they are also traveling during the daylight hours when traffic is heavier.

The second peak period is May when the fawns are about to be born. Prior to this time the does' last year's fawns are still with them. As their birthing time approaches, the does become territorial—the only time that whitetails are territorial—and they drive the yearlings away. Being thrown on their own for the first time, these young deer wander about in unfamiliar territory, and many are killed on the highways.

Also, acorns have been falling since mid-September and acorns are a deer's favorite food. On most back roads the right-of-way is usually sixty-six feet. This means that many of the tree branches are hanging over the road. Super-highways have such wide rights-of-way that the trees are set back a hundred feet or more from the road, thus the deer eating the acorns from those trees are not in or near the road.

Any oak growing along a back road is going to have more branches on its road side than it will have on the woodland side because the road exposes that side to more sunlight. Plants and trees grow toward the sun. Having more branches means having more leaves that produce more food, which allows for a greater production of acorns on that side of the tree. Therefore, any oak growing along a back road will drop more acorns in the road than in the woods, and the deer and the squirrels are in the road picking them up.

Bucks are active for no more than four to six hours per day if they are gathering food under good conditions. During the rutting season, however, the bucks travel almost constantly searching for receptive females, and that increases their chances of being killed by a factor of four. Ordinarily, bucks exhibit extreme caution in going about their activities, but many of them become downright careless during the rutting season—and that increases their chances of being killed.

I think it would be safe to say that an adult buck's chances of being killed by an automobile during the rutting season would be ten to twelve times greater than it would be during the rest of the year.

I N *DEER & DEER HUNTING* **magazine an article written by Randall Schwalbach purportedly debunked the claim that sonic whistles help to prevent automobiles from hitting deer. For the past several years you have been selling a deer whistle called the Sav-A-Life Deer Alert in your catalog. What did you think of the article and what do you honestly think of deer whistles?** *K. S., Stillwater, New Jersey*

I thought the article was one that was needed, and it was an attempt by the magazine to bring to its readers the latest facts on all aspects of deer and their

Being alert for eyeshine can help prevent deer-car accidents at night, as can using a deer whistle on your car.

behavior. I would have liked for the various testing agencies to have been more objective and to list the various whistles by name and company instead of grouping them as "they." There are a number of inferior products on the market. I do know that the Sav-A-Life Deer Alert performs in the sound range claimed by its manufacturer. Every product listed in our L. L. Rue catalog is either manufactured to our specifications or has been tested and is being used by my son and myself.

Before we decided to handle the Sav-A-Life Deer Alert I did months of extensive field testing. I did not use the scientific instruments that the researchers used. I do not know at what kilohertz a deer can hear. I do know that the deer can hear the ultrasound produced by the Sav-A-Life Deer Alert whistles, and up to distances of 300 feet. I know this for a fact because I have personally witnessed it in tests I have made.

Right after I first put the whistles on my vehicle I was driving from Blairstown to my home. A car preceded me by about 300 feet. There were two six-month-old fawns, feeding in a hayfield, that paid no attention as the first car went past. As I approached, I "blew" them away. Both fawns brought their heads up, looked in my direction, and dashed away. Farther up the road six does and fawns were grazing about 300 feet from the road. They paid no attention to the first car, but all raised their heads as I approached. I have had deer approaching the road stop, turn around, and dash off. I have had deer that were standing on the shoulder of the road leave it before I got there.

These are all personal observations. Is it all coincidence? I think not. I honestly believe that the Sav-A-Life Deer Alert works based on my own experience with them.

I live in an area where the deer population is estimated at over thirty-five deer to the square mile. I have in the past been involved in twelve car-deer accidents. I do drive defensively. On the rural back roads that I travel constantly to and from my home I always drive down the center of the road and at night I keep my high beams on, dimming the lights and getting over in my own lane at the first indication that a car is approaching from the opposite direction. I constantly watch for "eyeshine" on the shoulder of the road. When a doe crosses the road I watch for her two fawns to cross after her. I have always driven like that and I still had the twelve collisions. Now I also use the Save-A-Life Deer Alert whistles; since I began using them I have had no accidents.

I HAVE RECENTLY **returned from a hunting trip in the northeastern area of Colorado where I was hunting for mule deer near the South Platte River. Although this is a plains area and the mule deer is considered more of a foothills or mountain deer, some really large mule deer heads have been taken in this area. The thing that surprised me was that I saw more white-tailed deer than I saw mule deer. This was not so several years ago when I first hunted there. Are the whitetails forcing the mule deer out?** *J. L., Wheeling, West Virginia*

The white-tailed deer are definitely increasing in numbers over most of the eastern portion of Colorado because they are increasing both their range and their numbers in most of the western states and in the Canadian prairie prov-

When competition for habitat occurs between whitetails and mule deer, the mule deer are often pushed into open areas where they are easier marks for hunters.

inces. The whitetails are following up the river drainages of the South Platte, the South Republican, and the Arkansas rivers. The brushy river bottoms provide the whitetail with the type of cover that it needs to thrive and survive.

The mule deer used to frequent these bottoms, but as the whitetail numbers have increased, the mulies have moved out onto the more open areas. The Fish and Game Department figures that there currently are between six and eight thousand whitetails in the state, and probably more. It is known that there are now more whitetails than there are mule deer along the South Platte. The hunters, however, annually take more mule deer than they do whitetails because the mule deer are more visible in their open areas. The lopsided harvest of the two deer will also help to expand the range and the population of the whitetail as more and more mule deer are taken.

Not only have the whitetails become more numerous, some of them have become huge. In 1978 Ivan Rhodes took such a monster buck in Yuma County near the Bonny Reservoir. This was the first buck from Colorado to ever make the Boone and Crockett record book. He scored $182\frac{5}{8}$ points and shared the

72nd spot with a whitetail from Virden, Manitoba. (In the latest edition of the Boone and Crockett book this buck has been pushed back to the 104th spot. Another Colorado whitetail scoring 175⅞ now ranks 343rd.)

I ATTENDED YOUR **white-tailed deer seminar here in Indianapolis a few years ago and someone asked you a question on mule deer. In your answer you mentioned something about not seeing as many big mule deer in Yellowstone National Park as you did years ago. Just recently I read a book put out by someone working in the park stating that the range in Yellowstone is better now than it used to be. If the range is better now than it used to be, why aren't the deer there as big as they used to be?** *P.O., Indianapolis, Indiana*

You have asked exactly the right question, and it's the same one that I ask: If the habitat in the park is supposed to be so much better, why aren't the deer bigger?

Not only am I not finding the big mule deer bucks that I used to find, I'm not finding nearly as many mule deer, period. This is not my observation alone; just ask any of the professional photographers who congregate in the park. I have asked dozens.

I fully realize that all of these professional photographers are my direct competitors, but most of them are also my personal friends. Although they probably would not tell me exactly where they saw a huge mule deer buck, nor would I ask them, they aren't seeing them either. If they were seeing big mule deer bucks, they would be photographing them, and I would see the pictures appearing above their credit lines. I don't.

The truth of the matter is that the elk population has increased so dramatically in Yellowstone in the past decade that they are actually destroying the mule deer's habitat.

Years ago the elk during the rutting season were commonly found around the Madison River, Elk Park, Norris, Willow Flats, and Swan Lake Flats. I never saw a bull north of Golden Gate. Now bull elk and their harems are found almost to the town of Gardiner. In the winter the area surrounding Mammoth used to hold six to eight of the biggest bulls, with never a cow to be seen. Now there are elk cows and their young by the hundreds in that region, with never a big bull to be seen.

The increased population of the elk herd has devastated the vegetation in the Mammoth area. This area was always a major mule deer wintering area.

Mule deer have difficulty in areas with large elk populations because the elk can reach much more vegetation than the mulies can.

IRENE VANDERMOLEN

However, the elk can reach and eat everything that a mule deer can reach and much higher. Yes, there are some mule deer in the Mammoth area, but not as many as there used to be, nor do any of the bucks get antlers as large.

Actually, the park officials would like to see a tremendously severe winter occur that would cause a thousand or so elk to die of starvation, as they surely would. This would solve part of their problem without their having to make any decisions that might cause controversy.

The park officials are in the midst of a controversy right now about the reintroduction of the wolf to the park. The reintroduction is being fought by ranchers on the outskirts of the park, and I can fully understand their concern. However, we must consider the greater good to the entire park's ecosystem. The park is trying to exist as a natural area, and it cannot do so without the larger predators, such as the wolf and the cougar, being present. I strongly support the reintroduction of both of these predators to Yellowstone. I also strongly support a payment system to the ranchers for any *proven* livestock losses caused by these large predators.

The predators could reduce the number of elk, which would reduce the unremitting pressure the elk put on the vegetation. If the vegetation could recover, and it could take years, we would in time see big mule deer bucks in the park again.

I READ SOMEWHERE that they are getting quite a number of hybrid deer — crosses between the whitetail and the mule deer — in the province of Alberta. Do the two species usually interbreed?

O. H., Minneapolis, Minnesota

Under most circumstances the two species do not interbreed, but they can. Usually the two species don't even intermingle when groups of them are feeding in the same area. However, concrete evidence exists that the two species do interbreed and the reports of its occurrence are increasing. There is also evidence that the offspring of such hybridizations are fertile, although sometimes they are not.

The interbreeding between the two species usually results from a mating between a white-tailed buck and a mule deer doe. This is because of the differences in the breeding behavior of the two species. Both of the males chase after the doe, but the whitetail is much more persistent, chasing the doe farther and faster, even when she is accepting his advances. The mule deer buck chases after the doe, but if she is not ready to be bred and she runs off, he quits. Both bucks start to chase the doe before she is actually in estrus. If both bucks chase the same doe, the whitetail will always win out because he outlasts the competition.

Mule deer and white-tailed bucks have been seen fighting on a number of occasions, with the mule deer, being heavier on the average, probably the victor. There is one record of where both bucks lost; their remains were found the following year with their antlers still locked from a battle the previous fall.

Externally the hybrids show an intermingling of characteristics. The antler tines may come off the main beam, as do those of the whitetails, but the tips of the tines may fork, as do those of the mule deer. However, I find that these characteristics can be very misleading as I have seen a number of whitetail antlers from New Jersey and Pennsylvania that have the tines forking at the tips. And these were from deer that had been taken from areas where no mule deer have ever been.

The tails of the hybrids have the shape of the whitetail and are white underneath. The top of the tail is all black like that of a black-tail, a subspecies of the mulie. Again, this is not a sure-fire characteristic, as I have photographed whitetails in Virginia that had the entire upper tail surface black.

I have long stated that the best way to make positive identification of the various deer is by checking the size and placement of their metatarsal glands. The metatarsal gland of the whitetail is a small, round gland found below the center of the foot, closer to the toes. The mule deer's metatarsal is a long slash above the center of the foot, closer to the heel. The hybrid's metatarsal is shorter than the mule deer's, longer than the whitetail's, but like the whitetail's, it is more oval. It is located slightly above the center of the foot.

Experimental breeding has proven that if the female offspring of these hybrids are bred back to a mule deer over successive generations, their offspring will lose all whitetail characteristics. Within three or four generations they will have completely reverted back to being mule deer. Conversely, the same results would occur if the young were bred only to whitetails; their characteristics would dominate. I know of no such breeding program. It is probably occurring in the wild, as the white-tailed buck is much more persistent in breeding behavior.

The mule deer population is being drastically reduced in both Saskatchewan and Alberta. This is primarily occurring because more of the wilderness areas are being opened up. So, basically, the tremendous expansion of the whitetails' range in these provinces—and the whitetail is now being found at the 6,000-foot elevation—is being fostered by man's altering the environment. What may be less evident is that a portion of the mule deer population may be

Although mule deer bucks are generally heavier than whitetail bucks and more likely to win a fight, they are not as aggressive in pursuing does in the rutting season.

LEN RUE, JR.

assimilating into the whitetail population through the interbreeding of the two species. This is also happening with the desert mule deer in Texas. Biologists believe that in time the whitetail will breed the desert mule out of existence.

Poachers beware. Through the science of biochemistry and a process known as an electrophoresis all meats can be positively identified by the protein bands in their cells as seen through the electron microscope. The protein bands of the whitetail and the mule deer are distinctly different, and yet the characteristics of both appear in the meat of the hybrids.

I**F DEER AND turkeys eat the same foods, won't an increase in turkeys cut down on the deer herd?**   *T. L., Shamokin, Pennsylvania*

I**N SOUTHWESTERN WISCONSIN where I live and hunt, the wild turkey has been reintroduced. The turkeys have been very successful, with flocks of over thirty birds being sighted. Scouting for deer this year I have noticed large areas where turkeys have scraped away the ground cover and eaten the acorns. Also, I have noticed turkey tracks in the cornfields after the harvest. Since corn and acorns are two choice deer foods, how much are the deer and turkeys in competition and what effect could this have on the deer population in this area?**

R. N., Onalaska, Wisconsin

Additional information just crossed my desk recently: In Texas the harvest by hunters of white-tailed deer increased by approximately 15 percent in 1981–82 over the previous year, while the wild turkey harvest has set an all-time high.

Concern over the competition between deer and wild turkeys is one that has been voiced by many people. So much so that the game departments in Virginia, Pennsylvania, and Vermont have done research into the matter. It is true that turkeys and deer both feed on corn, acorns, beechnuts, and other similar foods. However, the research has shown that these two species are not in enough direct competition to be a limiting factor on either of the other's population. This conclusion was arrived at because deer and turkeys eat enough different foods, or foods that are not available to the other, that the competition has been minimized.

Our white-tailed deer herds are constantly expanding both in range and in numbers. It is now estimated that there are over nineteen million whitetails in

North America north of the Mexican border. This is probably the highest number of whitetails ever to inhabit our continent.

At the same time, the wild turkey range and numbers have also been skyrocketing. Wild turkeys are being, or have been, introduced or reintroduced to all of the contiguous forty-eight states and the southern tier of the Canadian provinces. Forty-six of our states now allow spring turkey hunting.

I mention both of these facts to prove to you that even without the research studies that have been done just the mere fact that the population and range of both species is steadily increasing shows that they are not serious competitors. Anyone who lives in a deer area that now has a huntable population of wild turkeys has the best of both worlds.

I ATTENDED YOUR **white-tailed deer seminar in Springfield, Massachusetts. You advocated clear-cutting blocks of woodland, where it would not cause erosion, as a means of producing an abundance of nutritious deer food. You said that burning the remaining branches and brush after the timber or the firewood was removed would return nutrients to the soil faster.**

I am an avid bow hunter in the fall, but I am just as avid a turkey hunter in the spring. Wouldn't your plan of clear-cutting and then burning the brush be detrimental to the turkeys even though it benefited the deer? *E. J., Albany, New York*

It is true that turkeys are usually found in mature or maturing woodlands because they feed heavily on the mast crops that such woodlands produce. It is equally true that turkeys also need cleared, grassy areas in the spring so that the poults can find the insects that are the mainstay of their diet. There are usually far more insects in a grass field than in the woodland.

If large areas were clear-cut, it would also be detrimental to the turkeys because I have found that they seldom will feed more than 150 feet out in the open away from protective cover, and usually less.

The first year after clear-cutting and burning, both the deer and the turkeys will benefit from the resurgence of grass and other vegetation. From the second to about the tenth year or so the area will produce a bonanza of food for the deer but will probably be avoided by the turkeys because they shun extensive, brushy areas because predators are too easily hidden there. Even in fairly open areas I have found that the turkeys will walk around a brushy patch, rather than through it, to avoid predators.

After the tenth year, in most circumstances, the brush will grow beyond the deer's reach as the brush grows into the beanpole stage. These saplings will begin to form a solid canopy that will shade out the understory vegetation, reducing its value almost completely to the deer. It will be of little value to the turkey, as well, because until some of the young trees are killed by their competition for sunlight they will be spaced too closely to allow the turkeys the freedom of movement they require.

If the beanpole trees are birch, maple, and aspen trees—trees that produce no mast crops—they will be of little value to either the deer or the turkey, although the deer will feed on the fallen maple leaves. If they are oaks, hickories, beech, or other mast-producing trees, they will begin to bear nuts after fifteen to twenty years and will be of benefit to both the deer and the turkey.

I AM BOTH a turkey and a deer hunter and I hunt both with a bow. The turkey population in the area where I hunt has been good for quite a while and our deer herd is now recovering nicely, although we still don't see many bucks with good racks. I have noticed that although deer and turkeys both inhabit the same area, they don't mix very well. When deer are feeding in an area and a turkey flock comes into the same area, the deer usually move out. Why?   *B. A., Barre, Vermont*

Your experience doesn't coincide with mine. I have seen turkeys and deer feed in the same area, but I would not say that it was done amicably. It has been my experience that the turkeys usually left the area first because I have seldom seen turkeys feed in one spot for more than fifteen or twenty minutes, no matter how much food was available. I have seen turkeys leave an area that had food to search over an area that had little or no food. They just don't stay in one spot very long while feeding.

It has been interesting to see the interaction between the deer and the turkeys because at different times one or the other was the aggressor. I have seen adult deer chase turkeys from the food area by striking out at the birds with their front hooves, exactly as they would chase off a rival deer. At other times I have seen adult turkeys chase young deer away from food by flapping their wings at them. In no instance did I ever see the act of aggression carried out to a point of making actual body contact; it was always done more as a threat gesture.

I don't believe that the deer like to feed in the same area as the turkeys because the turkeys are so noisy while feeding. The deer dislike the scratching that the turkeys do in feeding, either because it attracts attention to them or it foils their ability to detect the presence of a possible predator.

I WAS INVITED **to go bow-hunting by a friend of mine who lives in the southern part of Georgia not far from the Florida border. It was really out in the boonies and real wild with all that long moss hanging on the trees and palmetto growing all over. It looked like a great place for snakes and I think I spent more time looking out for them than I did looking for deer. I only felt safe when I was up in my tree stand. We hunted for four days and I saw lots of deer, but didn't get to kill a nice buck until the last evening. On the third day I saw a really big-rack buck, but before it got close to me it was spooked off by a couple of wild hogs. That really surprised me because the hogs weren't all that big. I'd say about 80 to 100 pounds, and the buck was at least 135 to 150 pounds. When I told my friend about this later he said that the deer were afraid of pigs and would run off every time. He also said that I really didn't have to be too concerned about snakes when I saw pigs because the pigs will eat the snakes.**

My questions are these: Why are the deer afraid of the wild hogs or pigs? Do the pigs eat the snakes and, if so, why don't they get poisoned when the snakes bite them or when they eat the snakes?

W. B., New York, New York

I don't know why deer are so afraid of feral pigs, but I do know that they are. And the pigs don't even have to be big ones. One winter I got a real education on just that down in Texas. One ranch that I was at had good white-tailed bucks, but they also had collared peccaries, or javelinas. I would say that the biggest peccary boar I saw didn't weigh much more than 50 pounds, 60 at the most. Yet every time the peccaries were in the area the deer would leave.

I was photographing on another ranch where we had baited for the deer and two feral pigs came in. In no time flat the deer were gone. Whenever we stepped out of the blind the pigs would take off. When we got back in the blind the pigs would come back. As the rancher wanted to get rid of the pigs, and I wanted to get deer photos, I borrowed a rifle from him and killed one of the pigs. The other was gone before I could shoot again and it never did come back.

I can't imagine peccaries ever attacking a deer, nor can I imagine the feral pigs doing that either. If it were in the mountains of Texas or North Carolina where they have the big European wild boar, that would be different because those boars get to be well over 300 pounds in weight.

Usually peccaries are in small groups of six to ten animals or more, and feral pigs also travel in groups. I know that the feral pigs would eat a newborn fawn if they found one. Pigs readily eat meat, preferring it when possible to get it. I don't know if the peccaries would attack a fawn or not, but they are wild pigs. The deer's fear of the feral pigs and the peccaries may be an instilled fear from the time when they were fawns.

It is a proven fact that all kinds of pigs will eat whatever meat they find or can capture. Snakes, poisonous or not, are just so much grist for their mills.

The pigs seem to be immune to the venom of poisonous snakes. However, I suspect that because most pigs usually have a layer of fat under their skin it is not likely that the snake's venom could get into their bloodstream when they are bitten. Even when the pigs eat the snake's head and the poison glands the poison would end up in the pig's digestive system and to be effective it would have to get into its bloodstream.

When a pig grabs a snake it chomps down with its jaws, breaking the snake's backbone. It then twists its head violently from side to side, flailing the snake around like a piece of soft rope.

ANY INFORMATION YOU **can give on protection against rattlesnakes in central Kentucky during early bow season would be appreciated since they have been found in our hunting area.**

B. P., Harrodsburg, Kentucky

Anyone hunting in areas where the chances of encountering a poisonous snake are good should definitely take a few simple precautions. You just can't be constantly worried about encountering a poisonous snake and still enjoy yourself while hunting.

I don't hunt in snake-infested areas, but I do hunt snakes. Years ago I bought a pair of Gokey snakeproof boots, which is one of the best life insurance policies I ever bought. Wearing these boots I have actually caught big Texas diamondback rattlesnakes by pinning them down with my foot. The boots are knee high and the snakes simply can't bite through them.

There are a number of different kinds of leggings being offered made out of solid metal, metal screening, plastic, leather, or nylon. Several companies also make chaps out of 1,000-denier nylon, a weave so tight and strong that a snake's fangs cannot penetrate it. I prefer the chaps over the leggings, and the ones I wear are made by the Bob Allen Company. With both the chaps and the leggings you must wear a heavy shoe or boot that at least covers the ankle.

Great care should be exercised as to where you walk, sit, or put your hands. It is important to know that the poisonous snakes hunt at night and are apt to be active when you walk to your tree stand in the early-morning darkness. During the daylight hours the snakes will seek shade when the temperature rises above seventy degrees Fahrenheit. A snake can only strike about a half to a third of its total body length and usually it is less than a half. You actually have to be very close to a snake for it to be able to bite you.

When working in snake country I always carry a snakebite kit. Today, many authorities are recommending a smaller version of the electric "stun gun." The electric shock localizes, or minimizes, the effect of the venom on tissue. I personally have had no experience with this piece of equipment, and I don't know anyone who has. I do feel it is worth looking into, however.

OVER THE PAST **few years I have seen a couple of television programs on wolves and have read a number of newspaper and magazine articles on them. It all has me a bit confused. Some of the articles claim that predators sanitize the area by taking only the old, the crippled, the sick, or the young. Others claim that the wolf is responsible for the decline in the caribou herds in certain sections of Alaska. Some of the articles advocate complete protection of the wolves; others want them hunted extensively and bountied.**

As you probably know, we have the largest population of wolves of any of the lower forty-eight states right here in Minnesota. And we have hot arguments on how to properly manage the wolves. I don't want to see any animal exterminated, but I am a deer hunter. Are the wolves going to ruin the deer-hunting in the northern part of our state?

O. P., Minneapolis, Minnesota

I commend you for trying to get the facts, to hear both sides of the story. That is always my first recommendation: get the facts, then make up your own mind.

I do not know just how many wolves you have in your section of the country. I am sure that the state management of the wolves is the correct one for your state, since much of the earliest work on the wolves was done by David Mech, who works in Minnesota and is one of the top wolf researchers in North America. I would not attempt to make suggestions to him, nor for any area that he has studied. I can, however, offer some personal observations that I have made on wolf behavior.

The wolf, the coyote, the cougar, any and all predators, are creatures of opportunity. They take whatever they can, whenever the opportunity presents itself. The members of the cat family do not have the choices that the members of the dog family have because the felines are basically stalkers, while the canines are coursers. A single healthy wolf would have a very difficult time catching a single healthy caribou, but a pack of wolves can usually take most prey species.

One time at Mt. McKinley I and dozens of other folks watched two young caribou bulls repeatedly tease a solitary wolf. A number of times the caribou got so close to the wolf that he dashed after them, only to be lost in the dust as they ran off. They did this five or six times until the wolf tired of the game and refused to chase after them. He knew he couldn't catch the caribou, and they knew it too.

In the Cassier Mountains of British Columbia I saw a herd of about 400 adult caribou that had only two calves in attendance. There should have been at least seventy to eighty calves, but the wolf population was high and had practically eliminated the calf crop. In this instance they were acting as expected, taking the young because they were the easiest. However, a pack of eight of these wolves also took down the only really prime, peeled-antlered caribou bull in the entire herd. That was definitely the result of selective hunting.

Studies of cougars killing mule deer have shown that the big cats consistently take more of the big adult males than they do the does and fawns. Much of this is the result of circumstances. Mule deer bucks are usually found at higher elevations than are the does and fawns, preferring the rim rock country to the lower wooded areas. So do the cougars. The cougars just naturally encounter more adult bucks than does and fawns, and consequently most of their kills are of the animals they encounter most frequently.

Some friends of mine witnessed a pack of coyotes kill a mule deer buck in Yellowstone National Park. The buck and his harem were feeding on a side hill among clumps of sage. One coyote trotted up the ridge above the deer, in plain sight of them. While all of the deer watched the coyote on the ridge, three other coyotes sneaked up a gully below the deer. When the three coyotes were in place the coyote on the ridge ran directly down at the deer. The buck ran closer to the ambushing coyotes than the does did and the three of them pulled him down. In this case the buck was taken because he was the nearest to them; they would have taken a doe if she had been the closest.

I just read a fascinating report out of Montana. The study showed that the cougar and the coyotes killed prime animals, while the deer killed by automobiles were the old, injured, sick, or young. They reasoned that the animals in poor condition were at the lowest elevation and tended to find ease in passage when the snow was deep by walking on the roads. The prime mule deer fed higher and wintered up where they were subject to attacks by both cougar and coyote more frequently.

It is a known fact that with white-tailed deer the bucks have a tendency to stay on the periphery of the winter deer yards. Thus, any predator seeking prey in the yard is much more likely to encounter a buck before it would a doe or fawn.

As I said before, most predators tend to take advantage of whatever opportunity presents itself, whenever it is presented. One additional factor that plays an important part is how plentiful the food is and how hungry the predator is when it is hunting. An extremely hungry predator is going to put a lot more effort into its hunting than is one that is just moderately hungry.

Are the wolves going to reduce the deer in northern Minnesota? Definitely. Are they going to eliminate the deer? Definitely not. No predator wipes out its prey species; its own numbers are reduced through starvation or through reduced or eliminated breeding potential as its prey species declines.

ARE FOXES EVER **a threat to the white-tailed deer's fawns? I found some fawn legs at a fox den that I discovered.**   *J. S., Ames, Iowa*

I cannot say that foxes never kill fawns, but I will have to say that such an occurrence would be exceedingly rare. I know of only one authenticated case of a fox chasing a fawn. Perhaps the fox would have killed the fawn had it caught it.

The average weight of an adult red fox is only nine and one-half pounds, with fawns averaging five to seven pounds at birth. A fox could handle a newborn fawn but a four- or five-day-old one would be quite a job.

The fawns are born at the same time that the fox's main prey are also having young. In May and June there are lots of young rabbits, chipmunks, mice, ground-nesting birds, their eggs, and their young to act as buffer species.

The legs of the fawns you saw at the fox den were probably those that had been scavenged. Mortality by natural causes among fawns can be fairly high according to weather conditions, and other factors. Accidents to the fawns or to their mothers may cause the fawns to die. The bodies of these fawns, when found, would be eaten by the fox, and if the fox could carry the remains, they would be taken back to the den as food for the pups.

Part Four
Hunting Deer

IS HUNTING DETRIMENTAL **to natural selection of deer?**

T. W., Scranton, Pennsylvania

Your question prompted me to do a little research, and I found that twenty-three of the lower forty-eight states opened their rifle-hunting season before November 10 while twenty-five states opened it after that date.

The number of bow hunters is increasing in most areas every year, and they are becoming more proficient. The records bear that out as the kill ratio per hunter climbs. However, the greatest number of deer taken legally each year is taken by gun hunters.

Throughout most of North America the peak of the white-tailed deer's breeding season is the week of November 10 through 17. The actual breeding season extends from about the last week in October through all of November into the middle of December. The mule deer of the Rocky Mountains are a week or so later. I am fully cognizant that the deer in the Southwest breed even later, and there are some that breed earlier, but I still maintain November 10 through 17 is the peak week.

Using that as a basis, it stands to reason that the states that open their seasons before the peak week have to be depleting their herds of some of their best breeding stock.

The only reason that a buck deer has antlers is to prove himself dominant to the lesser bucks. Bucks that are at the top of the social hierarchy do most of the breeding, thus passing on their genes to the future generations of the deer.

Most hunters will always pass up a lesser buck to take a trophy buck. There are many hunters who will take only trophy deer. It is the trophy deer that are our most desirable breeders.

In some of the states the seasons are set early so that the hunters can get in

Shooting a buck won't remove his genes entirely from the gene pool if he has lived through at least one breeding season.

to hunt the deer before the deep snows and the cold of winter lock them out. For some states, such as California, it is traditional to hunt deer in the summer, but don't ask me why.

States that are opening the firearms season before November 10 are, in my opinion, removing some of their finest breeding stock. They are not, however, removing the trophy buck's genes from the breeding pool. Even though the trophy buck is gone, all the younger bucks he has sired have his genes and will pass them on when they breed. And every bit as important as the bucks' genes, maybe even more important, are the genes of the trophy buck carried by his female offspring. It is a biological fact that characteristics run from father to daughter to grandson. Does just don't get the credit they so rightfully deserve in the production of trophy bucks.

How can **I convince my wife that hunting is not cruel, that it is not a waste of time, and that it can be enjoyable? I'd like her to take an interest in hunting because I love it so. I'd even like her to hunt with me.**
M. W., Clifton, New Jersey

You have your work cut out for you, but it can be done. If your wife was born and raised in the city, you have a greater job than if she were raised in a rural area. In most rural areas hunting is a tradition in most families. According to Rutgers University's Eagleton Institute, the profile of the average antihunter is a teenage college girl who has been raised in an urban environment and who knows nothing about wildlife.

For starters you should try to interest your wife in deer. The best way to do this is to take her on drives into your hunting area in the summer when you start to scout for deer. Even the most rabid antihunters enjoy watching deer. If you have children, make deer-watching a family affair; start them early.

Show her all the deer possible; sit and watch their activities; explain to her what the deer eat, what they are doing, and why. Get her to read your copy of *Deer & Deer Hunting* magazine. There are a number of good articles by women, including some about women who hunt and why they do it. Get her to read my book *The Deer of North America* so she can be knowledgeable about deer. (I hope you have read my book previously so you can answer any questions that she might have.) With knowledge will come the understanding of why our deer herds must be controlled by hunting, of why starvation is a constant threat in the north.

When bow season comes take her out on your stand for the evening hunt. Don't wake her up early in the morning and have her stumble around in the dark for the morning hunt. If you don't bow hunt, take her out on only the best, the warmest days of gun season. Do not rough it to be a he-man; make it as easy, as comfortable, as enjoyable as you can. You might not mind standing out in a driving rainstorm, but don't expect your wife as a novice to do it. Outfit her in proper hunting clothes.

Take your wife only as an observer, not as a hunter, unless she expresses the desire to hunt. Then you will have to train her to be proficient in whichever weapon she will use. Practice, practice, practice with her, stressing the ability to make sure, clean, one-shot kills. With or without your wife, you also need to practice to make sure, clean, one-shot kills.

There are many women who hunt. Perhaps one of your buddies has such a wife or girlfriend. Make sure the two women meet. A woman almost always understands another woman's point of view better than a man does and the hunting woman may be a better salesperson for hunting than you are.

Always stress the beauty of the out-of-doors. Make her aware how much you enjoy the outing, even if you don't see a deer. Stress that killing the deer is what makes you a hunter but that just being in the out-of-doors is why you enjoy being a hunter. Explain to her that you never take a "chance" shot. If you don't think you can kill the deer with the first shot, you don't shoot. Explain the moral obligation we hunters have to the wildlife we hunt: to kill cleanly and not to inflict pain. If you hunt by that credo and expect the same from her, she will respect you for it and it minimizes the "cruelty" charge.

Show respect for the deer after you have killed it. Dress it properly and utilize it. Waste not, want not. A deer in the freezer can save a hundred dollars or more on your meat bill. Venison, properly handled, is a better, more nutritious meat for you than any you can buy at the butcher's.

And, if you want your wife to enjoy hunting and be with you, remember that it's a two-way street. If she wants you to take her to see a play in the city, do it. If she would like to go dancing, visit her mother, have you go shopping with her, do it.

By following these suggestions you might not only gain a new hunting partner but also might gain an even better marital relationship. And that ain't bad. Good luck.

I HAVE BEEN told that the antihunting faction tried to have bow-hunting banned in your state of New Jersey. I read and hear more about people who are antigun, antitrapping, and antihunting all the time. I live for my bow-hunting and I want my children to be able to enjoy it, too, when they are old enough. I love being in the out-of-doors just seeing the deer as much as I do hunting them.

I am a life member of the National Rifle Association (NRA) and I have joined the Virginia Deer Hunter's Association. What else can I do to insure that my children and future generations of Americans can enjoy hunting as much as I do? *B. L., Lexington, Virginia*

Education. There are, today, about 16 million deer hunters in the United States. That figure is probably low by about half because it represents licensed hunters that can be counted. We have approximately 247 million people. Deduct one-fourth of that total for children under eighteen and that leaves about 185 million adults. Deduct the 24 million hunters and that leaves about 160 million nonhunters for a ratio of about one to six. There is no doubt about it, there are more of them than there are of us.

As our country becomes increasingly urbanized, the nonhunters will make even greater gains at our expense. The bright side of the coin is that I have found that many of the urban people who are nonhunters are not necessarily antihunters. I also have to concede that the antihunters are exceedingly well organized, well funded, very vocal, and many of them, although misguided, have a very high profile and ready access to all of the media, which they use very effectively. You don't have to be right to be loud.

Our greatest defense, in fact our only defense, is education. I have long advocated that the game divisions of each state send speakers into our public schools to talk to the children, to give them the facts of life about wildlife and game management. We must reach, and we must teach, the children because they are the voters of the future; it will be their taxes that will have to help support management programs. To date it has not been this way since most management programs and land acquisitions have come entirely from hunters' license fees and from the Pittman-Robertson funds that are derived from self-imposed taxes on hunting equipment. With the numbers of hunters declining in many areas the loss in revenues will have to come from the general public. It has been proven that the general public benefits far more from access to state-owned hunting grounds than do the hunters who paid for such land. The general public has long given lip service to acquiring public lands and the proper management of these lands for the greatest benefit to game and non-game species and for the greater benefit of all people. It is time that these nonpaying users put their money where their mouths are, and it has to happen. We must educate the children because they are the taxpayers of the future.

When antihunting articles appear in the newspapers and magazines it

Everyone enjoys watching animals in their natural habitat. Getting your family and friends interested in deer could be the first step in creating an interest in hunting.

behooves us, as hunters, to properly, intelligently, and factually refute any errors by sending letters to the editors. On a number of occasions the major television channels have given distorted, self-serving views of hunters and hunting. Organized hunters should not only boycott the sponsors whose advertising paid for the offending program but also the networks themselves. Any drop in the Nielson rating hits the networks where it hurts—in the pocketbook. I am not against anyone's giving his own viewpoint; we are all entitled to that. What I do expect is fairness, accuracy, and the equal opportunity for our side of the story to be told.

We have just been given the most important fact sheet on hunting and game management that I have ever had the privilege to read. It is a twelve-page bulletin put out by the Connecticut Department of Environmental Protection entitled "An Evaluation of Deer Management." The publication was collectively developed by the New England chapter of The Wildlife Society and the Northeast Deer Technical Commission. All of the men who collaborated on this bulletin are professional wildlife biologists. The bulletin is the most concise, most fact-filled, most accurate compilation of deer information that I have ever read. Every hunter should read it for his or her own knowledge as well as to be able to refute the claims and statements of the antihunters. Most antihunters are misinformed about the true basics of wildlife and its management. We hunters cannot afford to be misinformed.

The bulletin explores all of the options available in game management and discusses their practicality and effectiveness. It covers the hunter's role, transplanting, fencing, repellents, fertility agents, supplemental feeding, predation, and so forth. This is must reading. It is available, free of charge, from the Connecticut Department of Environmental Protection, 165 Capitol Avenue, Room 243, Hartford, CT 06106.

I SUBSCRIBE TO **a half dozen sporting magazines and so often I read of the same men taking the biggest deer, the grand slam on sheep, or some trophy animal I never even heard of. I understand that the major difference between the European and the American systems of hunting is that in Europe the landowner owns the game and in the United States the state owns the game, no matter whose land it is on. Consequently, only the wealthy people can hunt in Europe.**

Is the same thing now happening here in the United States? Does the average hunter stand a chance of getting a trophy buck?

H. W., Minneapolis, Minnesota

People with money are always going to have privileges that are denied to the rest of us. They are going to have more time to hunt; they can go where they want to hunt; and they can afford to hunt the species that they want.

Big money allows the hunters to pursue big bucks; however, it doesn't guarantee that their bucks will get in the record books. This is the major difference between hunting trophy deer and hunting trophy animals in exotic places.

There are any number of ranches or preserves in this country that are doing their very best to raise big bucks, and they do raise some big ones. Only wealthy hunters get to hunt there, but very seldom are the deer really big enough to make it into the record books.

The wealthy hunters can afford to fly back into the remote corners of exotic lands and take trophy animals. There is seldom real competition for these animals; the lessened hunting pressure allows the exotic animals to live long enough to become the trophies that are achieved only with age.

Hunting trophy whitetails is as democratic as any hunting can be; the next world record may be taken by anyone having the time and the ambition that it takes to really hunt big deer.

The hunters, particularly deer hunters, that you see written up consistently in the sporting magazines are not rich; many of them live average lives and work at average jobs, at average wages. They cannot be considered wealthy in terms of money. But they are not at all average when it comes to hunting – they are truly dedicated deer hunters.

These men and women spend every minute that they can spare from their families and their jobs to study and learn about deer. They are out living with the deer, eating, sleeping, dreaming, talking, and making plans about deer. They spare no effort, accept all hardships, and work at it constantly to take only trophy deer. That such dedication pays off is substantiated by their trophy bucks.

I agree with the recognition to the deer that comes with its entry into the record books. A perusal of the records will show what section of the country is producing the largest bucks, indicating what areas are best to hunt.

I agree with the recognition given to the hunter who shot the biggest bucks. Although some trophy bucks are taken by a fluke of luck, the majority are taken as a result of lots of hard work and of knowledge of the deer and its habits. Trophy deer didn't get to be trophy deer by being dumb; they survived by using all of their senses and accumulated wisdom. They don't even have the same habits as regular deer; most trophy bucks do not move around as much during the daylight hours as the regular bucks, despite the rut's being on.

I do deplore the recognition given to men with money enough to buy their way into the record books. The prices being paid today for some of the top trophies open the way for a veritable Pandora's box of abuses. Where money creates a demand there are always those who will fill that demand whether the trophy is taken legally or illegally.

The higher the prices go for truly trophy deer heads – and the price range is now from $5,000 to $45,000 – the less chance the average hunter has of ever taking such a buck. At those prices poachers are going to shoot every trophy buck possible before the season opens.

I UNDERSTAND THAT **December 1989 was the coldest December on record for Pennsylvania and that January 1990 was the second warmest we have ever had. Do those types of conditions mean that deer hunting will be better the next fall?**　　　*P. V., Scranton, Pennsylvania*

You are absolutely right. As I sit writing this in February 1990, it is raining outside and the temperature is forty-six degrees Fahrenheit. Our temperatures are averaging ten degrees or more above normal and that, not Rolaids, spells relief for our deer herds.

The 1989 acorn crop was spotty across North America. Here in New Jersey only some of the red oaks had any acorns. There were no white oak acorns at all. In some of the other states in which I lectured the acorn crop was good. I know your area of Pennsylvania did not have an abundance of acorns.

Despite the shortage of acorns the deer in our area went into winter fat as pigs because our farm crops were good and most of our deer depend on the crops, not on browse. You didn't mention where you hunt. If it is the southern half of Pennsylvania, the deer would also be in good condition because the crops were good. If you hunt in the northern, wooded tier of counties, the deer had to be in poor condition because much of that area is overbrowsed, and there are few farm areas and little or no acorns.

Winter 1989 came in with a bang in December and although the snow was not deep, it stayed powder dry because the temperature did not get above freezing for over three weeks. The wind driving that cold air down out of Canada was fierce. If those conditions had continued, our deer losses would have been very high across the northern part of the United States. Fortunately for the deer, and the deer hunter, the weather changed.

I predict that 1990 will see a substantial increase in the deer herd across the nation because the survival rate of the deer will be exceptionally high, more fawns will be born, and the fawn mortality rate will drop. I predict that heavier-bodied, larger-antlered bucks will be taken in the fall.

I HAVE HEARD **it said that it is harder hunting deer in the southern states than it is in the North. Do you have any opinion on this?**

L. C., Newport, Rhode Island

I sure do! One fall I hunted in South Carolina on a twenty-thousand-acre tract managed by Deer Unlimited. There were lots of deer there, and some big ones were taken, but it was a doe day that allowed me to score.

It isn't that it is physically harder hunting in the southern states, it's just that there are so many factors against success. First of all, the seasons are longer in the South with some of the states having an open season of three to four months; that's three to four months of harassing those deer compared to one to three weeks in the northern states. Those deer get to be a lot more wary of man.

Second, there are many more times the amount of vegetative cover than we ordinarily have in the North. Also, in the North we often hunt in snow, which helps to make the deer stand out from its background. In South Carolina they had not yet had a frost when I was there and it would have been next to impossible to even see elephants.

Third, there are not as many hunters to the square mile in the South as there are in most regions in the North; the deer just hide out at the first sign of danger and there are not enough hunters to keep them moving.

Fourth, the weather is hotter and the deer are in their winter coats. No deer in its right mind is going to move at all when the sun is up when it could just as well feed under the cool cover of darkness.

The fall when I was there I was further handicapped by the fact that it was the week of the full moon. The full moon, combined with the hunting pressure, would guarantee that the deer would feed at night.

Yes, I would have to say that it is a lot harder hunting deer in the South under those conditions than it would be hunting deer in the North. Several hunters at the camp while I was there were from Pennsylvania. They hunted in South Carolina because, as they said, to get their deer there they really had to hunt.

RECENTLY I MADE a trip into the city to buy some pressure-treated lumber that would ultimately be used to construct a portable deer stand. The building-supply store was located directly across the street from a pork-processing plant and the odor that dominated the area was a mishmash between pleasant and awful. I made a comment about the odor to the man who was loading my lumber and he said that he never even noticed it anymore. Apparently his sense of smell had adjusted itself so that the odor was no longer unpleasant, or even noticeable for that matter.

On my way back to my camp I began to wonder if deer noses work the same way as ours. If they do, then why wouldn't it be feasible to leave a recently worn article of clothing on each visit to my stand? Certainly the deer coming to feed would eventually get used to the scent and it would not spook them any longer. *H. T., Swansboro, North Carolina*

Your idea is interesting, but it doesn't work quite that way. As I have often mentioned in my deer seminars, deer are not panicked by the odor of man because they encounter it so often. It's the *fresh* odor of man that alerts the deer, causing it to use avoidance tactics.

For example, a man walks through the woods around 3:00 P.M. A deer coming from its bedding area to its feeding area at 6:30 P.M. encounters the faint odor of man. The deer also encounters the faint odor of the farmer who cultivated the corn in the field that the deer plans to feed in. The deer also encounters the odor of the farmer's dog, which had accompanied the farmer to the field and which left when the farmer did. Now all three odors are of man and dog but they are faint and the odors of the farmer and the dog are where they are expected to be. The deer has undoubtedly encountered these same odors in the same spot before. The deer would be alert, but would go on to do its feeding.

On another day the same man walked through the same woods, but this time at 6:00 P.M. The farmer and his dog had stayed late because the work needed to be done in that particular field on that particular day. The same deer coming from his bedding area to the feeding area now encounters the fresh odor of the man who had walked through the woods. Its nostrils and senses are assailed by the cloud of dangerous odor that hangs in the air. There is no way that that deer will continue on its regular path to the field.

The deer may or may not even attempt to feed in the field. If it goes to the field, it will go by a circuitous route, not its normal route.

On reaching the field the deer encounters the fresh odor of the farmer and

Of the five senses, the most important to a deer is scent. Hunters are far more detectable when they smoke, wear deodorant or aftershave, or have a strong smell like gasoline on their clothes.

his dog. There is no way that that deer will enter that field. It knows that the farmer and his tractor are harmless but that the dog represents danger. That deer promptly decides to feed elsewhere.

Now you plan to introduce, and then replace, an article of clothing heavy with your scent each time you go to your stand. The first thing that you will be doing is introducing man's odor where the deer may not be accustomed to finding it, out in the woods between the deer's bedding and feeding areas. This will definitely alert the deer and, if the odor is fresh, it will alarm the deer so that it will avoid the area that day.

Each time you put out a new article of scent-saturated clothing you alert and alarm the deer again. After this happens two or three times the deer may completely abandon the area.

The man at the lumber mill didn't notice the odor because it was constant; it permeated the area. Deer are not afraid to browse the shrubbery along the side of a house because the house is always there, doesn't move, hasn't hurt the deer, and the odor of the house and its human inhabitants permeate the area.

Your introduction of your scent-laden clothing is not a constant. Unless you and your clothing live at your stand constantly you are an introduced odor that will always alert, and probably alarm, the deer right out of the area. Don't do it.

H

OW HIGH IN **a tree should a deer stand be placed?**

N. O., Easton, Pennsylvania

The height of the tree stand has to be determined by the amount of hunting pressure the deer are subjected to. Under normal conditions a stand placed

Tree stands give a new perspective to a photographer as well as to a hunter.

LEN RUE, JR.

twelve feet above the ground would be above the regular sight plane of a deer. Ten to twelve feet is high enough so that your scent will dissipate easily.

Twenty years ago I used to say that eastern deer did not look up, although western deer did because of the predators such as the cougar. Today the eastern deer are subjected to far more predation from trees in the form of bow hunters than any western deer ever experienced.

Facetiously, I say that our eastern deer are wearing their hoof tips off tripping over rocks because they are always looking up into the trees.

In areas of average hunting pressure I would suggest at least a twenty-foot height, and for extreme pressure thirty feet or more.

HOW SOON AFTER **I put up a tree stand can it be used?**

T. O., Atlanta, Georgia

I don't know what the laws are regarding permanent tree stands in your state. Most states prohibit the use of permanent tree stands unless they are built on your own private land. If you are talking about permanent tree stands, I would recommend that they be built as early in the summer as possible to allow them to weather. As you may or may not know, I camouflage everything and if I were to put up a permanent stand, I would paint the stand in a camouflage pattern so it would blend in with its surroundings and not be noticeable. By putting the tree stand up early the smell of the paint and the fresh lumber would be gone long before the hunting season.

If you are talking about using a portable tree stand, then it depends on the weather. If the day is warm and the thermals of air are rising, then the stand can be used immediately. If the day is overcast and damp, you don't have to worry about the odor of your tree stand; your own body odor will be flowing downward like water pouring out of a pail.

IUSE A **tree-climbing stand for deer hunting. I had one that was easy to use and comfortable to sit in, but it had me facing the tree. This was okay for gun-hunting, but it was too much of a drawback for use in bow-hunting. The stand I now use has shock cord holding the stand in place and fastened to my feet as I climb. The main problem is that I often only have a short time to hunt and I can't help but make**

noise when I climb the tree using the stand. Do you think that I'm driving the deer away from my hunting area by using a climbing stand?

C. O., Erie, Pennsylvania

Any unusual noise may frighten the deer out of the area that you are hunting. If you have only a short time to hunt, there probably is not enough time after you have your tree stand in place for the area to quiet down and return to normal. If you are hunting along a trail leading from a feeding area to a bedding area, any deer you scare off may be the only ones using that particular trail at that time.

I have used both types of the climbing stands you mentioned. Climbing a tree with them is noisy. I prefer using a nonclimbing stand and screw-in tree steps to get in and out of the stand. Where possible I would recommend leaving your stand in place. Unfortunately, I fully realize that many tree stands are stolen. Paint your stand in camouflage colors, chain it fast to the tree with a substantial chain, use screw-in tree steps, and remove the bottom six steps when you leave the tree. That way, when you plan to hunt you merely have to use the same holes you made with the tree steps the first time. This will save you lots of time and is practically noiseless.

W**HAT ARE YOUR views on ladder stands? I am presently thinking of having one made with materials that I have on hand. Do you think that hunting from a ladder (say twelve to fifteen feet) rather than with a portable nonclimbing tree stand lessens my chances of bagging a trophy buck? Would a trophy buck notice a camouflaged ladder stand quicker than a nonclimber so that I might not be able to get off a shot? It seems that every time I read about a trophy buck being killed it's not from a ladder and I just want to know how effective a ladder is in the woods.**

Also, I live in southwestern Louisiana and have heard different people's views about when the rut begins. What can you tell me?

G. F., Southwestern Louisiana

No, I do not believe that the deer will notice the ladder stand. From personal observation deer seldom notice anything that is not moving. And you did say that the ladder would be camouflaged, which I heartily endorse. I wear camo at every opportunity and I camouflage all of the equipment I use.

The reason most hunters don't use ladder stands is that they are bulkier and heavier to carry than the traditional tree stands. They are a lot easier to use and to put up, however.

If you are hunting in an area that is heavily hunted, a ladder stand may not get you up high enough to be above the deer's line of sight. Twelve to fifteen feet is fine as long as the deer are not exceptionally wary. Where heavily hunted I would suggest that you be at least twenty feet or more above the ground. I have used stands that were thirty-five feet in some of the southern states where the deer are heavily hunted months on end.

Northern Louisiana is about on the thirty-third parallel. South of that line the rut for white-tailed deer is about six to eight weeks later than it is north of that line, with a gradation of time on either side of the line. In your area of Louisiana the deer's rutting season should start around the last of November or the first of December, with most of the deer being bred the last of December and the first week in January. Two years ago I saw two does bred on January 5, and the rut, chasing, and fighting was at its peak.

I HAVE BEEN watching a large white-tailed buck that I believe to be the dominant buck of the area I hunt. I have also located a trail used regularly by him. There are two trees along the trail that could be hunted from. One is directly above the trail (I would have to shoot straight down) and the other is off to the side of the trail (I would have to shoot broadside at the deer). I believe I could easily hit my mark from either tree. The prevailing wind is in my favor from both trees. Which tree would offer a more deadly shot with bow and arrow?

D. I., Menomonee Falls, Wisconsin

I would recommend that you take the broadside shot. A large white-tailed buck, as seen from above, has a rib cage width of about twelve inches. From that width you would have to subtract about three inches for the hair, skin, and ribs on each side of the lungs. It is true that a shot through the deer's spine would drop it in its tracks but, at most, that is a one-inch-wide target if hit dead center. A shot through the lungs would also be fatal, even though the buck would run off when hit.

Shooting at the deer broadside provides a much larger target of at least twelve inches high by eighteen inches in length. A shot through the heart, lungs, or liver would be fatal, even though the buck would run off when hit. If your arrow were to go high, it might hit the spine, dropping the deer in its tracks. Go for the broadside shot.

A deer standing broadside provides a large target; nevertheless, good aim is crucial. If you don't hit a vital organ, the deer will be able to run away but may suffer a great deal.

WHEN HUNTING FROM a tree stand approximately ten feet above the ground, and a deer approaches within forty yards, where should the cross hairs be centered? I have been told to compensate for the height of the stand from the ground and aim high on the upper shoulder rather than directly at the shoulder in order for the bullet's path to hit vital organs.

Could you please resolve this question? This same situation happened to me on the opening day of the 1986/87 buck season.

F. M., Allentown, Pennsylvania

More important than the height of your tree stand, which is only ten feet at a forty-yard distance, is the distance that you have your rifle sighted in at, plus the caliber, plus the bullet weight. If your rifle is sighted in for forty to fifty

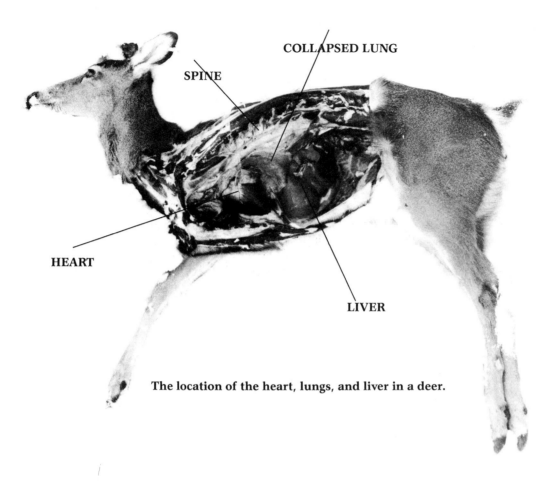

COLLAPSED LUNG

SPINE

HEART

LIVER

The location of the heart, lungs, and liver in a deer.

yards, I would aim precisely at the spot you want to hit because the angle you are shooting is only causing the bullet to drop one inch for each foot it travels, which is minimal.

As most rifles are sighted in for one hundred yards, such as a 30-06 using a 180-grain bullet, you would be shooting .06 inches high at forty yards because of the compensation you made for gravity when you sighted the rifle in.

There has been too much folklore told for too long about undershooting up a hill and overshooting down a hill. Gravity is gravity is gravity and the bullet will drop no faster or slower going up or down a hill than it would on the level. In the case of extreme steep angles the angle that the bullet enters the deer's body will have some effect on its hitting a vital area. If your gun is properly sighted for the distance you are shooting, and you have the ability to hold the rifle steady, the bullet should hit where you aim.

W

HAT GEAR DO **you take with you when you go hunting?**

C. W., Manchester, Tennessee

That's one of the shortest letters I've ever received and I wish I could be as brief with my answer, but I can't.

I do not hunt in wilderness areas so I do not need a compass and a map. In either bow- or gun-hunting I carry just about the same gear so I'll mention what I do take and why, and then make suggestions for those hunters who do go back into unfamiliar territory.

To start with I *always* wear, or have with me, certain items that other people do not usually carry, but will need when hunting. I have spent most of my life in the back country and the following items, to me, are essential.

I always carry a sheath knife and, being right-handed, I wear it on my left hip. I started this as a kid and have gotten so used to having it there that I feel naked when I don't feel the knife's handle under my left elbow. Although you can easily gut and skin a deer with a much smaller knife, I prefer a six-inch blade. My knife is a tool that allows me to slice up through the deer's rib cage with ease and to do other heavy-duty chores.

In my seventeen years of guiding in the Canadian wilderness I always carried a marble match safe. Now, in warm weather, I usually carry a propane lighter. However, propane lighters do not work well in cold weather as the fuel will not expand to create the needed gas. You should always carry something with you, however, to start a fire if needed.

On my belt I also carry a champion Swiss army knife. This is my tool kit. I always have need of the screwdrivers, the pliers, and particularly the saw blade. All of you have had to remove some small branches that would have blocked a good shot from your stand. The Swiss saw blade removes them easily.

In my left hip pocket I always carry a six-foot length of one-quarter-inch parachute shroud cord. I first got into the habit because I needed the cord to lash my paddles to the thwarts so I could use them in portaging my canoe. I use it for hundreds of purposes, and you will too. Once you get in the habit of carrying such a cord you will wonder how you ever got along without it.

In either my hip pocket or a shirt pocket I carry about twenty sheets of toilet paper for the times that they are absolutely essential. In my left front pants pocket I carry a pair of nail clippers and in my right front pocket a tube of lip balm for lips dried by sun, wind, or cold. In my shirt pocket I carry a ballpoint pen and note paper for keeping notes or starting fires.

You will need a license unless you hunt on your own land. I never heard of a bow hunter forgetting his arrows because most use bow quivers. However, if using a gun, you will need ammunition of the right gauge or caliber. In bow-hunting I always dress in Trebark; in gun-hunting in New Jersey you have to have at least 440 square inches of blaze orange, so my blaze orange vest is a must. And, of course, your bow or gun.

I always carry the rest of my gear in a daypack and I am now using one made of "quiet cloth." The first thing that goes in is an emergency space blanket. I always carry one in my photo vest and would not think of going anywhere in the out-of-doors without one. This small piece of heat-retentive fabric could save your life and works great as an emergency poncho to save you from getting wet in a storm. If there's a possibility of showers, I carry a poncho. A pair of lightweight rubber slip-ons to wear over your shoes will help cut down on leaving a trail of human scent, gasoline, and so forth.

A pair of small, powerful binoculars is a must in rifle-hunting where game must be identified at a distance and are a pleasure for use in bow-hunting. Also, bring along a small flashlight to use going to and from your stand.

I use Rue's white-acorn scent in September and/or a musk scent up until the middle of October, a sex scent during the rutting season, and fox scent as a cover scent at all times. Although using deer scents is not as important in rifle-hunting where many hunters make drives for their deer, the use of scents in bow-hunting is a must.

I have a cable deer-puller to use in sliding my deer if I am fortunate enough to get one. Several paper towels are in the pack to wipe my hands with after I have gutted the deer. I always have a couple of granola bars to snack on and a plastic jar for water. If I am to be out all day, and I seldom am, I carry a thermos of tea or cider, according to the weather, and sandwiches.

If you are going to hunt in back country that is unfamiliar, you should have a compass and know how to use it. You would need to have a topographic map of the area and know how to use it with the compass. You should have additional emergency food with you. You should carry a lightweight Qualofill sleeping bag and cover in case you are forced to spend the night in the woods.

If the weather is warm, you may want to take a mesh deer bag to put on your deer to keep the flies off the meat after you get it to the car.

I AM WRITING you this letter because I am puzzled by a response you gave to a reader in the November 1988 issue of *Deer & Deer Hunting* magazine. The question was this: "What gear do you take with you

when you go deer hunting?" In your response to this question you didn't mention anything about deer calls. Why? Is it because you do not believe in them? If you do use one, do you use it during both bow and gun seasons? What is the best call to use early in bow season?

P. R., North Troy, Vermont

Believe it or not, it was the sin of omission on my part. Yes, by all means use deer calls. One of the best deer calls on the market today is marketed through Helping Hunters. Not only does it imitate the grunt of a big boss buck, but by changing the location of the O-ring the same call can be used to make a high-pitched bleat that is especially attractive to does.

Bucks grunt primarily in the rutting season. They usually grunt as they track the does, while tending an estrous doe, and prior to and during their fights. The grunt call should always be used when you try to rattle in bucks.

The bleat call is effective all year long, and although it works best on does, it also will call in bucks in the fall.

I strongly believe in using calls, and I use them frequently in my photography. The fact that I did not mention them was pure oversight on my part. I hope I have now set the record straight.

WHICH TYPE OF camouflage is best?

O. R., Chillicothe, Ohio

For early bow-hunting season, when most of the vegetation is green, I would recommend the green-brown combinations. Later in the fall I would suggest the tan-brown combination, to match the turned or fallen leaves. When the leaves are off the trees Trebark is unquestionably the best. When there is snow on the ground, the white camouflage with black streaks is best.

Even if you have to wear blaze orange, use blaze orange camouflage that is a broken pattern. The broken pattern is what is important; you don't want an unbroken block of any color.

I'VE HEARD THAT deer perceive blaze orange as white and that it really stands out and is very noticeable to them. It appears as a solid block of color, a color that is not an integral part of the color scheme of nature during the hunting season. If this is so, what do you think about

Camouflage clothing helps you blend in while hunting, taking photographs, or scouting.

the requirement to wear blaze orange hunting clothing? It is hard enough to get a deer as it is, without having my clothing working against me.   *W. D., Clinton, New Jersey*

It doesn't matter what I think about the law requiring New Jersey hunters to wear 400 square inches of blaze orange during the gun season. It is the law and must be obeyed. It has definitely been proven that the accident and fatality rates have dropped dramatically in every state that has passed such laws. The saving of a single human life is worth far more than all the deer you will ever shoot.

Deer see their world in shades of gray, and to see exactly what they see just look at a black-and-white photograph of a scene. Blaze orange stands out as a light shade of gray. Where possible use blaze orange camouflage because then you will not have a solid block of this light shade. Even more important than wearing the blaze orange camouflage is training yourself to stand still. My years of working with deer have convinced me that they will not see you or be alarmed by you, even if you are wearing blaze orange, as long as you do not move. Most hunters move about almost constantly, and it is this motion that gives their location away quicker than the blaze orange will. Deer's eyes are especially sharp at detecting the slightest bit of motion within their range of vision, and they can see 310 degrees of a 360-degree circle.

Except during the gun season I always dress in camouflage – Trebark where it is appropriate – because this minimizes my being detected by the deer if I do move, or by other bow hunters and photographers.

I TOOK AN eight-point buck by using the tarsal glands from a three-point buck that I had shot in the bow season as an attractant. It came running and snorting at me through the woods with its head held ready to fight. I've told other hunters this story and have gotten mixed views about using the tarsal glands to attract bucks during the rut. What are your views?   *N. M., Jr., Fowlerville, Wisconsin*

CAN YOU USE **the tarsal scent glands of the deer as an attractant and how would you prepare them?**   *S. B., Nashville, Tennessee*

Yes, I did this for years. The tarsal scent glands are the most important scent glands a deer has. The glands can be removed either before or during the time

White-tailed buck urinating on his tarsal glands.

that the deer is being skinned. As there are very few blood vessels in the area, there is very little chance that you will get blood on the skin that you cut off. All you need is the skin, not any of the meat or tissue that lies beneath. The glands do not have to be prepared in any special way. To try to tan the skin chemically would spoil the glands' usefulness. Just hang them up on a piece of string in the shade and let them dry. Don't handle the glands any more than you absolutely have to. When you go hunting take them with you and either hang them up where you want the buck to stop or hang them on your stand as a cover scent. If you put the glands in an airtight plastic bag and keep them in your freezer, they will keep until the following year. They can be used for an entire bow-hunting season. As they are exposed to air, they will lose their effectiveness rather rapidly because no new scent is being produced nor is any urine being deposited on them. Because of this loss of scent they are seldom useful for more than just one season.

I LIVE ON **on a horse farm in southern Ohio and I am planning to deer hunt on the land behind my house. My area is rural with little farmland and a lot of wooded areas. The land I'm hunting on is private and has not been hunted for about ten years. I ride my horse through the woods about once every month. I am wondering if horse manure would be a good cover scent to hide my odor from the deer. I am also wondering if it would be better to ride my horse through the woods more often to let the deer become more familiar with the smell of horses. Do you think this will work?**

The land I hunt on has a high deer population with many main trails. Usually every evening I walk to a field where I have seen deer feeding and I watch for them. Will the deer be affected enough by my visits that they might quit feeding here or possibly abandon the area?

M. D., Kitts Hill, Ohio

Horse and cow manure are some of the best cover scents you can get. I recommend that bow hunters wear a light rubber boot after they get out of the car and have walked into the woods. Wearing these lightweight rubber boots masks odors, such as gasoline, that are probably on your leather boots from driving. I recommend that hunters, wearing these boots, walk through every cow flop or heap of horse manure that they can find on the way to their stand. If these domestic animals are in the area, the deer readily accept the animals themselves as being natural components of the environment, and their manure is a commonplace substance that the deer encounter frequently.

I would suggest that you ride your horse whenever you go to check on the deer because your horse is so readily accepted.

As a kid on a farm years ago, I rode on horses all of the time. By riding bareback I could lie down along the horse's back and practically become a part of it. In doing this I found that I could ride in among the deer, or at least get within fifty to sixty feet, the distance at which they will tolerate the presence of the horse. I tried to approach from downwind to minimize my human odor; however, I found that the deer seldom paid that much attention to my odor. I found that I could not sit upright and get close to the deer. Try it; you should have lots of fun and in the process you will learn a lot about the deer.

I do not suggest that you hunt from a horse and *do not* shoot your gun from a horse. Riding your horse during the hunting season could get both you and your horse shot, and very few horses are trained to resist bucking or bolting upon hearing the discharge of a firearm from a close distance.

WHICH IS BETTER **as a cover scent, fox or skunk?**

J. N., Zeeland, Michigan

I use red fox urine as a cover scent because the fox is not a threat to the deer; the two species share the same habitat. As the fox goes through its territory, it urinates on every projecting stick or clump of grass along its route, proclaiming ownership of that area. It's much like your dog urinating on all your car's tires—it is proclaiming to all other dogs that your car is part of its territory. Because of that habit deer are constantly encountering the smell of fox and it poses no threat to them. Fox urine has an acrid odor, we call it the "reek" of fox, which will help to overpower, overlay, or mask human odor.

Skunks discharge their scent only when they are threatened; it means danger to any animal encountering it. Deer read, and heed, the alarm, as well as the danger calls of other birds and animals. I would not use skunk scent as a cover scent.

IN *DEER & DEER HUNTING* **magazine I read an article about an author who used cow urine to attract bucks. Do you think this technique really works? If so, why or why not? I have taken a doe and three bucks with a bow, and I have not used any kind of lure. Do you think a lure would attract bucks?**

R. B., Humble, Texas

That author used urine from a cow in estrus, not just plain urine. When a cow, or a doe, is in estrus the estrogen in her system causes pheromones, which are scent molecules produced by her sexual organs, to be secreted with her urine. It is these pheromones that excite and stimulate the male so that he is most anxious to copulate, and to impregnate, the female. That function is the buck's reason for being.

Cows, sheep, goats, and deer are all ruminants; they are all related. It has been proven a number of times that a domestic cow in estrus will sexually attract bull moose. In all probability the sexual odor of all estrous ruminants is very similar in chemical origin, composition, and odor. Yes, it should work.

Wild animals, particularly deer, live in a world of scent. Although you have been very successful so far, I feel that your chance of continued success would be greatly improved by using both attractant and cover-up scents. Using any of the good scents should raise your chance of continued bow-hunting success.

IS IT POSSIBLE **to make an artificial scrape that bucks will come to?**
B. D., Hayward, Wisconsin

Yes. Scrapes are made by a single buck but are usually utilized by any buck passing through the area. You can scrape a shallow depression so that it looks like a buck's scrape, but it will not be used unless you add the magic ingredient—scent.

Most mammals live in a world of scent. Smell is the deer's most important

If you make a scrape that looks and smells natural, bucks are likely to use it.

LEN RUE, JR.

sense. It is the one they depend on to tell them the whereabouts of their enemies, it is how they locate food, and it is how they locate mates.

Scrapes are made by bucks as a means of communication. The scrape is used by many other bucks and does as they communicate with each other. It's more like a chain letter than a name card. Everyone gets involved.

Bucks mark their scrapes with feces, urine, and ejaculations. To make an artificial scrape work you must saturate it with a good sex scent. There are a number of good scents on the market but I recommend the Helping Hunter's sex scent.

Once the scrape has been established with the sex scent, the deer will add their own. Then the scrape is no longer manmade, it's a deer's scrape. It just happened to have been started by man and where man wanted it. The ingredients are all natural deer scents.

RATTLING ANTLERS TO **call in bucks seems to be increasing in popularity and I'd like to try it. Where can I buy a good set of antlers? I have tried the plastic antlers that are offered for sale, but they just don't sound right.** *T. J., Minneapolis, Minnesota*

WHAT IS THE **best time of the year to try rattling antlers?** *W. C., Ames, Iowa*

Tom Flemming, the "rattling man," proved to me that deer can be called in by rattling antlers. I know that it has been done for years in the Deep South but Tom proved it to me in Virginia on land that had lots of hunting pressure.

Rattling works best in areas where there is a high buck/doe ratio. Rattling can work any time during the rutting season, which is roughly from October 20 until December 15. The very peak of the rut, from November 10 to November 25, will also see the peak of response of the deer to rattling.

I agree, the plastic antlers just don't sound right. They aren't made of the right material, and they don't have the resonance or crack that real antlers have. The only person I know who sells "rattling antlers" is Gary Knepp, at R.D. 2 Box 261D, Newport, PA 17074. He has them in all sizes, weights, and prices. He sells the real thing at a price comparable to the plastic antlers.

I HAVE BEEN to a number of deer shows and have seen demonstrations on how to rattle in a buck. Basically they all do just about the same thing—they start off by crashing the antlers together. Some of the guys crash them together time after time, others keep them together and just rattle them back and forth.

Just before our bow season opened here in Wisconsin I was doing some scouting. I had my stand up in a tree on the edge of a corn field where the deer come out to feed. Just before it got dark a young buck came out of the woods. I don't know whether he was a four-pointer or a six-pointer, but he had a small, thin rack. When I crashed the antlers together he jumped as if he had been shot and ran off about 75 feet and then stopped and looked back. I crashed them together a couple more times and he was gone! I thought he would at least be interested enough to check out what was making the noise. What did I do wrong?

P. T., Eau Claire, Wisconsin

What you did wrong was to scare the living daylights out of the little guy. When you crashed your antlers together he thought he had accidentally gotten

The size of the antlers you choose to rattle must be appropriate for the size of buck you hope to attract.

too close to a couple of big bucks. This would be particularly true if you were using large antlers to rattle with. From my personal experience I have found that using large, heavy antlers will call in big bucks, but that you will call in more bucks if you use smaller antlers. There is a very definite difference in the sounds of large and small antlers.

In areas where you do not have big bucks I recommend that you use a small set of antlers, or just tap the big ones together lightly. Here in New Jersey we just don't have many big bucks. From personal observation I have seen small bucks run off when a couple of big bucks started to fight; the little bucks wanted no part of the action.

If your area has mainly small bucks, I suggest you start off—with either big or small antlers—by just ticking them together like a pair of young sparring bucks would do. Then, if no buck shows up, put a little more effort into your banging.

You can add some raking of the ground and nearby bushes with the antlers if you want to, although this is not necessary. I have witnessed dozens of fights between deer, and although their feet were straining against the ground and their bodies might have knocked down some nearby brush, the main sound was that of antler rattling against antler.

C<small>AN YOU RATTLE</small> **in deer by using large pieces of dried bamboo? I read an article somewhere where the author said that's what can be used.** *C. Y., Ely, Minnesota*

You are likely to read almost anything. I have never heard of anyone using bamboo, nor have I tried it. Unless I do try it I will not know.

I have tried using a piece of plastic pipe with several balls enclosed and have had some luck with it. I have tried the artificial antlers with no luck, although I know hunters who have had good luck with them. To me the plastic antlers just don't sound right.

I do have two sets of real deer antlers that I use—a large pair and a small pair. I prefer using the larger set because they sound better to me and, as they have a much deeper tone, they sound as if larger bucks were fighting. This is important. The sound of larger bucks fighting will be more attractive to whatever larger bucks are in the area. Big bucks aren't interested in a couple of little guys banging away.

Old-shed antlers don't work as well as new-shed ones do. Antlers that have lain in the woods for several years lose both their weight and their density, and they don't have the right sound. Even antlers that were newly shed when you got them should be soaked in water for several days prior to their being used. The soaking will replace some of the moisture lost by dehydration and return the antlers to their original deeper tone.

I HAD A very unnerving experience last year and, frankly, it has affected my bow-hunting and even my being in the woods.

I was going bow-hunting and was putting my tree stand up with tree-screw steps. I had screwed the steps in and had come back down to get my stand. Just as I was about to step to the ground an eight-point buck came out of the brush and charged right at me. I had soaked my foot pads in a deer musk scent and the buck must have followed my trail. Luckily I heard him coming and was able to climb back up the steps that I had just screwed in. I couldn't get my bow because it was still lying on the ground. There I was, treed. When I tried to climb down the buck would snort and paw the dirt. Believe me, I only tried to come down that one time. He kept me up the tree for fifteen to twenty minutes before he finally left. Even after he left I was still reluctant to come down. I really had a case of the shakes.

My questions are these: Is this behavior unusual? Do you know of other people being charged by wild deer? I am most reluctant to even hunt any more. Am I being unreasonable? Was I in as much danger as I thought I was?

Were you in danger? Yes. An enraged buck can be a deadly adversary. Every year people are killed or injured by captive bucks, and every year people are threatened by wild bucks.

Yes, the buck's behavior was most unusual. It will probably never happen again, but it could. A deer in the rutting season is potentially dangerous to anyone, and most hunters don't take that into consideration. People without the knowledge of or experience with deer always underestimate their speed, strength, and agility. They shouldn't. That buck also may have been one that had been raised in captivity and escaped, or was turned loose, and he would be doubly dangerous because he would have lost all of his fear of man. Just recently I saw in a book on deer behavior two photographs of an aggressive mule deer buck that had treed a man and kept him up the tree for a considerable length of time.

In using scent for bow-hunting deer—and I believe that everyone should—I

Two views of a buck exhibiting extreme aggression. Bucks are easily excited in the rutting season, so using scent on yourself to attract deer can be dangerous.

always recommend that the hunter *not* put the deer scent on his clothing and that the hunter *not* use scent pads on his feet. Hunters shouldn't attract the deer to themselves. Instead, the scent should be used to attract the deer to your area. It can be used to attract the buck to the precise spot at which you want him to be, but I don't believe that the hunter should serve as the focal point for the deer's attention. You have just found out how dangerous that could be.

Yes, by all means go back to hunting. You will be a better hunter in the future because you have gained a lot of respect for your quarry. You do not need to fear that such an attack will happen again. In all probability it never will.

MOST DEER THAT **are hit with an arrow run off and have to be tracked. Can a deer be dropped in its tracks with one shot?**

T. E., Peoria, Illinois

Yes, a deer that has been hit in the brain or in the spinal column will drop in its tracks. A brain shot will kill the deer instantly. A severance of the spinal column will drop the deer but will seldom be lethal. It will take a second shot to a vital organ to kill the deer.

The brain shot is an exceedingly difficult one for any hunter, and if the deer is a trophy animal, it should be avoided.

The spinal shot is the one most offered to bow hunters when the deer is directly under the tree stand. It is not a shot that should be tried by hunters on the ground. Most bow hunters have a tendency to shoot a trifle high. Any elevation of the arrow aimed at the spine will result in a complete miss.

WHILE BOW-HUNTING HERE **in Pennsylvania I missed a shot at a nice eight-point buck. He was not a huge animal, but he had a nice rack with about a sixteen- to eighteen-inch spread. He came to about sixty feet from my tree stand and stopped, standing broadside, checking the wind as if he had caught my scent. I put my sixty-foot pin on the middle of his chest and let go. Just as my arrow got to him he dropped low and the arrow went right over his back. I'll grant you that my shot would have been a little high, but not high enough to miss a broadside buck at sixty feet! Did the buck see the arrow coming, or did he hear the bow twang? How did he know to drop low instead of just running off? I hope you can shed some light on this because it sure has me puzzled, and it cost me a nice buck.** *E. L., Bangor, Pennsylvania*

Because the deer was suspicious to start with it was geared up to move quickly, and its reaction time was at a minimum. An unsuspecting deer would have taken longer to react.

It is a normal reaction for a deer to lower the body when it is surprised, alarmed, or threatened. They usually do this to gather themselves before leaping. Human speed-runners start from a crouched position using starting blocks. When the gun is fired they spring upright and off they go. By being in the crouched position they can run or jump farther when they release all their energy to the muscles. Most animals do the same thing instinctively. When the deer dropped, preparatory to dashing off, it lowered its body and you shot over it.

What triggered the deer to dash off can be only speculation. The deer would have seen something rather than have heard it because of the difference in the speed of light compared to the speed of sound. The deer may have seen you draw the bow, may have seen you release the arrow, or may actually have seen the arrow start its flight. The twanging of the bow string would occur only after the arrow left the string and was well on its way to the target.

I have seen deer drop, as you describe, many, many times and I have also seen it shown in several hunting videos. This is probably the number one reason for missing deer by overshooting. Hold lower on the body the next time.

I ATTENDED YOUR **white-tailed deer seminar in Holland, Michigan, and was very interested in your comments about how successful New York State's "deer search" program has been. The D.N.R. (Department of Natural Resources) here in Michigan opposes using dogs to track down wounded deer. Don't you think that it would be a good idea if our state, too, used dogs for tracking deer? Look at all the venison that would be found that would otherwise be wasted out in the woods.**

P. G., Holland, Michigan

Yes, I am all for any type of program that helps a hunter recover the deer he has wounded. Far too many deer are wasted each year because the hunter loses the wounded deer's trail or because he simply does not follow the trail far enough. Many of us simply aren't capable of following a wounded deer's trail. I, for one, can't see as well as I used to, even when I wear my glasses. I can't see the faint indentations made by the hoofs, I don't notice the overturned leaf, and I miss seeing a spot or splatter of blood.

In New York State the members of the Deer Search Club usually use long-haired dachshunds and the dogs are always worked on a rope or chain. The dogs are not used for deer hunting; they are used only to search for deer that have already been wounded. If the deer is only superficially wounded and can run off when it is located, the use of the dog is discontinued.

I was brought up living the maxim of "waste not, want not" and I still try to live that way today. In my opinion, every state and every hunter should employ every and all methods to recover or dispatch seriously wounded deer. It is a moral obligation on our part to fully utilize the creatures we hunt.

How do you feel about using dogs to hunt deer?

H. V., Altoona, Pennsylvania

In most sections of the country it is unethical, illegal, and reprehensible to use dogs to drive deer. In most states most hunters would shoot any dog seen chasing deer. Although I cannot condone shooting a dog, I do condemn anyone who has a dog and allows it to run loose. Feral, or wild, dogs have become so commonplace that they are now a threat to humans and domestic livestock as well as to all forms of wildlife, especially deer. It is not just the feral dogs that run deer, but many well-fed pets do it just because they are dogs. Dogs may

Even a well-fed domestic dog may attack a deer.

LOU STOUT

have been domesticated for ten thousand years or more, but they are still basically predators. Wild dogs are wild predators; pet dogs are potential predators. Domestication, like civilization, is only a thin veneer.

However, in some sections of the continent, such as in the white-cedar swamps in Ontario and the cypress swamps of South Carolina and Georgia, dogs are the only way to move the deer out of the swamps. The swamps are so treacherous, and the vegetation so dense, that it would be impossible to get the deer out without the dogs. Using dogs does not guarantee success, either, because the deer are adept at avoiding the dogs and the water washes away the deer's trail. Hunters from other sections should not condemn the hunters who do use dogs. Where hunting with dogs is legalized, the states recognize that it is the only way the deer can be hunted.

A FTER READING AN **excellent piece by Rob Wegner in *Deer & Deer Hunting* magazine on following wounded deer, I know that you advocate following the deer at once. I have always been led to believe that I should hold back for at least a half hour after shooting a deer to allow it to "stiffen up." How long does it take for a deer to stiffen up? How long after a deer is killed is it still okay to use the meat?**

J. B., Elmira, New York

I have to agree with you that Rob's article on following the wounded deer was an excellent piece of research and was on a subject that really needed to be reviewed. It is why I constantly tell hunters that if you want to know the basics about deer, you have to read *Deer & Deer Hunting* magazine.

How long does it take a wounded deer to stiffen up? Wounded deer don't; dead deer do. A wounded deer may lose so much blood that it may not be able to regain its feet after lying down, but it does not begin to stiffen up until after it dies.

Between ten and twenty minutes after death a deer's eyes will get a greenish cast to them. After a half hour rigor mortis begins to set in and this will cause the deer to stiffen up. The rigor mortis will cause the legs to stiffen although the body can still be bent. The only time the entire carcass becomes stiff is if it freezes solid.

Depending upon the weather, body heat in a dead deer is retained for about three hours. Even in freezing weather when the legs and extremities are beginning to freeze, body heat can still be detected beneath the deer's front legs, in the armpits, for almost that length of time. So much for a deer's stiffening up.

How long the meat will remain edible depends entirely upon the ambient temperature. A deer's internal body temperature is about 104 degrees. A deer is a ruminant and in its paunch are billions of bacteria, microflora, and microorganisms that break down the ingested food and convert it into fatty acids and methane gas. Decomposing vegetation, whether in a deer's paunch or not, gives off methane gas, which causes a deer to bloat, or swell up.

If the ambient temperature is at or below the freezing mark, when the wounded deer dies the microorganisms will continue to work until the deer's body heat drops and the carcass begins to freeze. There will be some slight swelling of the paunch, but with the exception of the internal organs, such as the heart and liver, and the tenderloins the rest of the meat will be edible for a period of twenty-four hours or longer during severe weather.

If the ambient temperature is in the vicinity of forty to sixty degrees, as it is in most bow-hunting seasons in most places, the meat would still be edible if the deer were found in the early hours of the day after it was shot. The skin of the abdomen may have a slight greenish tinge, but if the night were cold, the organisms' activity would have been curtailed drastically. Discard all of the internal organs and meat.

If the weather is in the seventy to eighty degree range, the deer will spoil if not found and eviscerated within three to four hours. The skin on the abdomen will turn dark green, the area around the wound may turn purple, and the hair on the ground side of the carcass will begin to slip. Nothing will be salvageable as the flies and the bacteria will have already begun their work to liquify the carcass.

DO DEER FEEL **pain when they are hurt?**   *D. J., Indianapolis, Indiana*

Higher forms of life feel pain to a greater degree than do lower forms because of a more complex nervous system and the greater development of the brain. A frog can be placed in a pan of cool water that has been placed on a lighted stove and it will actually be killed by the hot water before it is ever aware of the heat.

Convolutions, or indentations, of the brain are usually used as a basis for determining intelligence. The deer's brain is smaller for the size of its body than is a human brain, and its brain is much smoother. Therefore, a deer is not as intelligent as a human.

All wildlife have a tremendous tenacity of life; they don't give up. They are more stoic, accepting hardship as a way of life. Because of these factors they have the capacity to tolerate more pain than humans.

But, despite this dissertation, deer do feel pain. As sportsmen it is our moral obligation to hunt without causing pain if it can be avoided and to put any animal out of pain as quickly as possible if we do inadvertently cause it. *Do not* shoot at any animal that you are not reasonably sure of killing cleanly. *Do not* exceed the ability of your weapon or yourself.

WHY DO DEER **stick out their tongues when they die?**

C. T., Neenah, Wisconsin

A deer doesn't stick out its tongue when it dies because that implies an action that would require effort. When death occurs, for most creatures there is a relaxing of most of the muscles prior to rigor mortis setting in. When this occurs deer, and most other creatures, lose all control over their bodily functions so that in death a deer will often defecate, and its tongue will fall out of its mouth.

I WOULD LIKE **to ask about a subject no one likes to talk about: the gut-shot deer. Nothing can turn a moment of ecstasy into shame quicker than to discover that your carefully placed shot has defied the laws of physics and drifted a couple of feet back into the deer. Opening up a deer to discover a mess can nearly turn one off from venison forever.**

I have several related questions on how to make the best out of a bad situation and, somehow, by my care of the venison redeem myself a bit.

Considering that a kill involves about an hour's drag and a two-hour drive home, just wiping out the deer doesn't give much peace of mind. Should the carcass be washed in a stream? Should I treat the carcass with something (salt, baking soda, vinegar, or hydrogen peroxide) to neutralize the effects of spillage? Is there any danger of salmonella? Are there health dangers involved in exposing my hands to stomach, blad-

der, or fecal material while gutting a paunch-shot deer? How about
hanging the deer for a week to tenderize it? Can I still hang it or should
it be cut up immediately?

Sorry to broach this sickening subject. My concern, though, is in
being responsible about the venison and giving it the best care under
adverse situations.   *P. N., Johnstown, Pennsylvania*

Bobby Burns used to say, "The best-laid plans of mice and men gang aft agley,"
and I say, "The best-aimed shots go oft astray."

I appreciate your courage in admitting that you, like all of us, don't always
hit where you had planned. Actually, I have seen more paunch contents
dumped into the deer's body cavity as a result of sloppy field-dressing than by
gut-shooting. In either case, it's not the end of the world, although it often
smells that way.

Any time the paunch's contents are dumped into the body cavity, from
whatever cause, empty out the cavity of all organs and spilled contents and
wipe it out with any material at hand, be it dead leaves or dead grass. If water
is available, by all means wash the cavity thoroughly. If this can be done as
soon as the deer is recovered, the paunch contents should not have had time to
taint the meat. If water is not available at the kill site, wash out the body cavity
at the first opportunity you have.

When I butcher a deer, and I've done untold hundreds of them, I trim off
every piece of fat and tissue and remove all bones. By using the methods that I
do no part of the meat that I eat could have possibly been in contact with the
contents of the paunch so the spillage will not affect the meat. You might want
to get my videotape on butchering deer for complete instructions.

I know of no danger to humans from exposure to the contents of the
paunch, bladder, or fecal material, providing you have no cuts in your skin.
Then an infection might result as it would by getting any dirt into the cut.
Washing your hands with water as soon as you can, with hot soap and water
when possible, and disinfecting the cut with hydrogen peroxide should suffice.

You can only tenderize meat if it is held under conditions where the temperature is between thirty-four and thirty-eight degrees Fahrenheit. Any colder
than that, the bacterial activity ceases so that the fibers are not broken down;
any warmer than that, the bacteria will speed up the process too fast and cause
the meat to spoil.

I just wish more hunters would display the moral obligation that you do, to
thoroughly utilize the game we harvest.

WHAT IS THE **best way to handle a deer's carcass if the days turn warm during the hunting season?** *O. J., Utica, New York*

All deer should be gutted as soon as possible after being shot. The body cavity should be propped open with a stick to facilitate cooling the chest cavity and to allow the body heat to escape from both sides of the carcass. If the weather is continuously cold, you have no problem except to hang the carcass where it cannot be stolen by a marauding bear. If the nights are cold but the daytime warms up, hang the carcass in the shade and enough cold from the night should be retained in the meat to hold it through the daytime.

You may want to cover the entire carcass with a mosquito-netting bag to prevent flies from laying their eggs on the meat when it warms up.

If both the day and night are warm, stop your hunting and get the deer to a food locker or processing plant. Taking the skin off the deer will help to retard spoilage but you will lose some of the meat all over the surface of the carcass as it dehydrates.

If you can't get your meat out and the weather is warm, you could skin and butcher your deer, place the meat in waterproof plastic bags, and submerge it in a cold spring or water, if available. Check with your game department before hunting and before you do the above since some states do not allow butchering of the deer in the field in order to prevent poaching.

RECENTLY WE WERE **bow-hunting an area where only does and antlerless deer could be shot. This is part of a game management program whereby they are trying to reduce the entire deer population before they do damage to the habitat. My buddies and I got two large fawns and one large doe. When we butchered the deer we were amazed to find the difference in the color of the meat. The meat on the large doe was a deep red, like a piece of beef, but the meat on both of the fawns was a whitish-gray color. What makes the difference, and is it always this way?** *E. P., Athens, Georgia*

Your comparing the big doe's red meat to a piece of beef is good because the pale-colored meat of the fawns can best be compared to a piece of veal, the meat of a calf.

Ordinarily the color of the meat depends on the number of blood vessels coursing through the meat. I would imagine that physiologically there are as many blood vessels in a fawn's meat as there are in a doe's. However, I have noticed in the hundreds of deer I have butchered that the largest of the fawns always have lighter colored meat than do their smaller counterparts. I have also noticed that especially large yearling deer have lighter colored meat than do the smaller members of the peer group. It seems that the faster an animal grows, the lighter the color of its meat but, scientifically, I do not know why this is so.

AT WHAT TEMPERATURE **should meat be aged, and for how long?**

T. C., Erie, Pennsylvania

The finest aged beef is held at a temperature of 38 degrees Fahrenheit for a period of six weeks. Meat can be aged at temperatures between 34 and 38 degrees. Aging is a process of controlled bacteria multiplication. When meat is frozen all bacterial action ceases. At temperatures over 42 degrees the bacteria multiply too fast and the meat spoils. Hunters who hang their deer outside to age are only kidding themselves. The meat freezes at night, thaws and heats up during the day, and the process is repeated for as many days as the deer is hung up.

The ideal method is to hang the deer carcass in a walk-in refrigerator. However, some states do not allow venison to be hung up in the same locker as domestic animals. If you do not have access to a walk-in, you can section your deer and put it in your home refrigerator and run the temperature down to 38 degrees.

If none of this is available to you, I would recommend that you process your meat as soon as the body heat has cooled down. Aging makes meat much more tender because the controlled bacterial action breaks down the meat fibers. If you can't do it properly, don't do it at all. Allow your meat to cool, process it, and freeze it.

IHAVE RECENTLY **become very interested in the saturated fat content and cholesterol levels of foods in my diet. I am aware that white-tailed deer venison is generally believed to be lower in fat (leaner) than commercially raised beef. Visual side-by-side comparison would**

Because deer are constantly active, there is very little fat between their muscles.

also support this belief. Can you provide any quantitative statistics on how venison compares with beef?

An American Heart Association publication indicates that a 3-ounce portion of lean beef typically contains 7.7 grams of fat. The specific breakdown further suggests, per 3-ounce portion, 3.7 grams of saturated fat (bad actors), 3.4 grams of mono fat, 0.2 grams of poly-unsaturated fat, 77 milligrams of cholesterol, and 177 calories of food energy.

I am a thirty-six-year-old professional, in good health (except cholesterol level), and a fanatic whitetail hunter. I also volunteer as a New Jersey Hunter Education instructor. I would appreciate any feedback you may have.   *D. M., Old Bridge, New Jersey*

Venison is one of the finest meats you can eat; it's what keeps me jumping over fences. All kidding aside, it is as beneficial as most of our domestic meats, or more so, in terms of protein, vitamins, and minerals. Venison has less fat and fewer calories than the same size portions of beef, pork, or chicken and it is higher in calcium, phosphorus, and iron. Beef is touted as an iron-rich food, and it is, but venison is better. Venison is also subjected to less chemical exposure and contains no growth-stimulating hormones.

Venison is a drier meat because there is practically no fat between the various muscles. Beef is a much juicier meat because the cattle are bred, and fed, to have large quantities of fat marbled between the muscles. It is this fat that is so injurious to anyone's health. Since I bone all of my venison, and break down the hams into individual muscles, I remove every vestige of bone, fat, and tissue. I have absolutely nothing but pure meat and nothing to ever produce a gamey taste.

Venison by nature is a tougher, stringier meat because deer have to depend on those muscles for survival whereas beef cattle do not. However, since I usually crockpot all of my venison roasts, they come out very moist and too tender to be carved with a knife. You cannot eat a better meat than venison.

The following chart was taken from the book *Food Values of Portions* by J. Pennington and H. N. Church (Harper and Row, 1980, 186 pages).

Food	Quantity		Calories	Protein		Fat		Calcium[a]	Phosphorus[a]	Iron[a]
	Grams	Ounces		Grams	Ounces	Grams	Ounces			
Beef										
Hamburger, fried	99.25	3.5	197	19.2	0.67	12.8	0.45	5.3	165	[b]
T-bone steak, broiled	99.25	3.5	247	25.2	0.88	15.4	0.54	10.5	181	3.8
Rib roast, cooked	99.25	3.5	132	12.4	0.43	2.9	0.10	3.5	95	1.5
Veal, loin chop, cooked	99.25	3.5	226	12.1	0.42	19.3	0.68	3.1	100	1.5
Lamb, loin chop, cooked	99.25	3.5	90	10.9	0.38	4.8	0.17	3.5	86	1.2
Pork										
Bacon, fried	99.25	3.5	172	6.3	0.22	15.7	0.55	4.7	77	0.7
Ham, fresh, cooked	99.25	3.5	111	17.3	0.61	4.1	0.14	3.1	129	1.1
Loin chop, cooked	99.25	3.5	183	15.1	0.53	13.1	0.46	5.8	118	2.3
Poultry (domestic)										
Chicken, broiled	99.25	3.5	151	20.2	0.71	7.2	0.25	14.0	200	1.5
Duck	99.25	3.5	326	16.0	0.56	28.6	1.01	15.0	188	1.8
Goose	99.25	3.5	322	28.1	0.99	22.4	0.79	10.0	265	4.6
Turkey, roasted	99.25	3.5	200	30.9	1.09	7.6[b]	0.27	30.0	400	5.1
Venison										
Roast, cooked	99.25	3.5	146	29.5	1.04	2.2	0.07	20.0	264	3.5
Steak, broiled	99.25	3.5	201	33.5	1.18	6.4	0.23	29.0	286	7.8

[a] In milligrams.
[b] Reliable data are sparse.

Part Five

Photographing Deer

C AN YOU RECOMMEND a commonly known, easily obtained, quality camera that I can use for taking pictures of wildlife? I am on a limited budget at this time ($600 for camera and lens combined), so I will be purchasing the camera through Sears or J. C. Penney. Because I am a beginner I am thinking about buying an SLR camera with a manual override. Most of my shots will be taken from 50 to 200 yards. Later on I would like to have a lens that reaches out to 600 yards. I could cover five or six deer crossings with one shot on railroad tracks and power lines. Could I get clear enough pictures using a 2X or 3X converter on the lens that I purchase now?

Can an amateur photographer sell wildlife pictures to deer-hunting magazines, or do they only use photographs taken by professionals?

R. H., Appleton, Wisconsin

There are a number of good, inexpensive camera bodies available in the $100 to $200 price range, such as Pentax, Olympus, Minolta, and Nikon. I would

Capturing a wild buck on film takes more than just the right equipment—it requires scouting, knowledge of deer habits, and a great deal of patience.

You can't plan a photo like this. Be constantly alert and prepared to take advantage of whatever you see.

Instead of photographing only beautiful poses, try to capture action and interesting behavior.

suggest that you try a Nikon FM2 body and the best 400mm lens you can get for around $400. I do not know if either Sears or J. C. Penney handles this equipment; I buy photographic equipment from photographic dealers because they have a larger supply and a better choice of equipment.

You are right in buying an SLR camera, and it should be manual rather than having automatic metering. The fault with automatic metering is that the camera may be setting your exposure by reading too much of the background or too much of the subject itself. If you got a reading off a wild turkey, the exposure would be wrong for the general photo.

The 400mm lens will do nicely at a 50- to 75-yard range; it will not do for 200 yards. You also will not get a lens to take deer photos at 600 yards. I don't recommend any lens longer than 600mm, which used with a doubler would be a 1200mm. Even with that size lens a deer at 1,800 feet will be a mere flyspeck on your photo.

It would be great to be able to cover five or six deer crossings from one spot. You can't do it and neither can I. You will have to concentrate on just one crossing or trail, and then situate yourself no more than 100 feet from where you expect the deer to be. If the trail is well used, fine; or you can bait the deer to a particular spot. I would suggest you work from a blind.

Amateurs become professionals by taking the photos that editors want and will buy. These are not photos taken at 600 yards. Editors will buy from whomever has the photo they need. That's what's great about the wildlife photography business: it is wide open to everyone. The results are determined only by skill and persistence. Good luck.

I AM SERIOUSLY **considering taking up wildlife photography and I would appreciate it if you could recommend a good camera and lens that I can use both in the field and for conventional use. I am only going to do this as a personal hobby. Thanks, and keep up the good work you do.** *M. C., Texarkana, Texas*

I would suggest that you get a black-body Nikon FM2 camera. This is an excellent mechanical camera that is really trouble free. A motor drive can be obtained at a later date if you find that you need or want one.

Instead of getting the standard normal 50mm lens, I would suggest that you buy the Nikon 55mm macro lens. You can use this as your normal lens and also use it for close-up work, which the standard 50mm will not do.

Next I would get either an 80mm to 200mm or a 70mm to 210mm lens. This is the lens you will probably use most often. It is a good intermediate telephoto lens.

When you feel that you need a longer telephoto—and you will, to photograph big game—I suggest that you get a 400mm lens. I recommend the

Tamron line, as their lenses are very good and less expensive than the Nikon lenses of the same focal length.

To further enhance your photographic capabilities I would suggest you get a 1.4X teleconverter and perhaps even the 2X teleconverter. The teleconverters should be made by the same company that makes the lens you intend to use them with. The 1.4X teleconverter used on the 400mm lens will effectively increase its focal length to 560mm. It will also change an F4 lens to an F5.6. The 2X teleconverter changes your 400mm lens to an 800mm and makes the F4 lens an F8. That is my basic equipment and it is what I suggest you use.

Wʜᴀᴛ sɪᴢᴇ ʟᴇɴs **is pictured with you in your column, "Rue's Views"? How much does it cost?**   *B. O., Charleston, Missouri*

The lens pictured alongside my column is a 600mm F4 Nikon. The large diameter of the front of the lens is needed to make it an F4. The larger the diameter of the lens, the more light it allows to strike the film; hence, we call it a "fast lens."

I paid $4,684 for that lens when I first got it about four or five years ago. As the U.S. dollar has dropped in value against the Japanese yen the price has increased to over $6,000. None of the photographic supply houses even list a price any more; they all say "call." That means the price is shifting every day.

This lens is not really suitable for deer photography, although it can be used. I use it primarily for small birds or animals, and it can be used with extenders.

For deer photography I would recommend that you buy the fastest 400mm lens that you can afford and get extenders by the same manufacturer that are designed for that particular lens. At the present time my main wildlife lens is the Nikon 200mm to 400mm F4 zoom lens.

Aˢ ᴀɴ ᴀᴠɪᴅ **bow hunter I spend a great deal of time in the woods, both during the season and most of the year when the season is over, taking snapshots of wildlife. But I want to upgrade my picture-taking from snapshots to quality wildlife photographs. Most of the photos I take are of white-tailed deer since there are at least a hundred or more deer in the five-square-mile area that I hunt and take photos in.**

My camera is a Pentax P-3 Auto with a Tokina 70-210 F3.5 zoom and a Tokina 500mm F8 telephoto fixed-focus lens. I have the tripods and the monopods, auto window mounts, and beanbags. I use Kodak Gold 200- and 400-speed film. Usually I shoot at sunup or a half hour before and under low light conditions. The problem I have is with aperture settings and exposure speed. The 70-210 zoom can be used in the auto mode or in the manual mode, but the 500mm can be used in the manual mode only. When I depress the shutter release a speed will flash in the viewfinder in the manual mode. Should I set the shutter speed to that or not?

I would appreciate any suggestions you may have as to additional equipment that would help me in the field.   *D. W., Des Moines, Iowa*

I am not familiar with your Pentax P-3 camera, but I do know the Tokina 70-210 lens. The Tokina 500 F8 is undoubtedly a mirror lens and I would sell that at once and get a 400mm F4 lens. The 400mm lens is the main lens used by professionals. I would suggest that you check out either the Tamron or Tokina lenses in that range. Then I would also buy a 1.4X teleconverter made by the same company as the lens you choose. A 1.4X teleconverter will extend either of those lenses to a 560mm, but you will lose one full stop of light, making the lens an F5.6.

It is very important that you buy the fastest lens you can afford, as each f-stop larger will allow you to shoot twenty minutes earlier or later than you could if your lens were one stop lower. The smaller the f-stop number, the larger the diameter of the lens and the faster it is. Lenses are rated as F2, F2.8, F4, F5.6, F8, F11, F16, and F22, with the lower number one full stop faster than the number above it. I use my camera in the manual mode at all times and would suggest that you do, too.

WHY IS HIGHER ASA film, such as 400, 1000, or Seattle Film World's 640, not used since this would seem to allow for the taking of pictures under dark forest conditions that an ASA 64 or 100 film would not. Is the clarity factor or graininess all that critical when more pictures could be taken under poor to adverse conditions?   *A. D., Mahopac, New York*

As a professional photographer I use the film with an ASA of 64 or 100 because they produce much finer-grained photographs, because of finer clumps of dye, than do the faster films. It is true that the faster film will allow you to photograph under adverse conditions, but such photographs will never be purchased by editors if they can get similar subjects, under similar conditions, on the finer-grained films.

IAM TWELVE **years old and I am very interested in photography. What kind of lens should I buy for photographing white-tailed deer? I have a Pentax K1000. What kind of film should I use in order to sell to magazines?**

Also, could you tell me how to sell my pictures to magazines? How do you know what kind of pictures they want? When you sell your pictures to magazines, do they want you to submit the actual prints or the negatives? *T. E., Crown Point, Indiana*

Almost all professional wildlife photographers use Kodachrome 64 positive transparency film because this is what the magazines need in order to make the separations that they use to print the photographs. When you submit photographs you send in the original transparency. Magazines are not interested in seeing photographic prints.

To find out what the various magazines want, you will have to do just what I do. Get several issues of the magazines that you would like to send transparencies to and then study them to see what each magazine is buying. For example, *Deer & Deer Hunting* uses primarily deer photographs, *Field and Stream* is heavy on fish, *Sports Afield* uses a lot of work of gamebirds and waterfowl, and *Outdoor Life* goes in for big game.

Do not submit photographs to any magazine without first writing to the art director, photography editor, or general editor. Tell them what you have and ask if they would like to see it. The magazines are not obligated to return any photos that they did not ask to see. Many magazines require that you send return postage and envelopes when you submit your photos.

As for lenses, I would suggest that you start with an 80mm to 200mm or a 70mm to 210mm zoom lens. If and when you can afford it, get a 400mm lens. Maybe your folks could combine your birthday and Christmas presents and get it for you, as they are expensive. The 400mm is the number one lens for photography of most big game animals, including deer.

I also suggest that you get my book *How I Photograph Wildlife and Nature*; it will answer most of your questions and give you the benefit of my forty-five years of photography experience.

DOES YOUR CAMERA **shutter noise scare the deer you are photographing?**
B. W., Altoona, Pennsylvania

I always use a motor drive on my camera so I not only have the shutter noise to contend with but also the sound of the next frame of film being advanced. The answer to your question is yes. At times it literally blows them away—one click and they are gone! On the other hand, and this happens more frequently, the sound of the camera click will make the deer more alert. And photos of deer that are not alert are useless. I often expose one frame just to let the deer hear the noise and to bring its head up, or around, so that it will look alert.

You must also realize—and I have said this many, many times—that most of my photography is done in areas where the animals are not hunted, such as in national parks, refuges, and preserves. Hunted deer would undoubtedly bolt away as soon as they heard the camera click, as they would do at the first click of a gun.

Some camera companies have experimented with manufacturing "blimps," large insulated packages that fit over the entire camera and lens, having holes for the lens, the viewfinder, and the controls. The idea is sound but it has not met with much success. The only company that I know of today that offers a blimp is Hasselblad.

WHEN IS THE **best time to photograph a deer that I've shot?**
B. T., Wheeling, West Virginia

I suggest that trophy photos be taken as soon as possible to prevent the green-eyed sheen that occurs about twenty minutes after death. Any blood should be wiped off the muzzle and mouth, and the animal's tongue should be pushed back into the mouth. If there is a lot of blood in the area, move the deer before photographing it or, if the animal can't be moved, carry in fresh snow, grass, or dirt to cover the blood.

I'VE ALWAYS ENJOYED **looking at your pictures of deer and thinking of what it would be like to shoot something like that. I've seen deer, but they are either does or they are running away. How do you see so**

Sequences, like this one of a deer bounding through the snow, are often appealing to editors. (See also the shots of a doe giving birth in Part Two.)

many deer and get so close to them? I live in Georgia and, as you know, there aren't that many big-racked deer here. I have seen pictures that you have taken of deer in the South, but I don't understand how you can take pictures of deer that look like they could possibly be record class — and hardly anyone is able to shoot such a wall-hanger.

Another thing I don't understand is how you can take pictures of big deer, but never be able to shoot them. Is it because you are able to overcome your temptation or because you do not carry a gun with you? When you are out there looking at deer with big racks, how do you feel toward the animals?   *D. M., Hepzibah, Georgia*

I do not photograph wildlife where it is hunted. That means that I photograph my deer in national, state, or county parks, on private farms, ranches, estates, or on land owned by power plants, munition plants, or hospital grounds. A great many of my photographs have been taken on a private estate of 180 acres where the deer are fed. There are no fences and the deer are hunted when they leave the area, so during most of the hunting season they stay on the estate. I photograph on Texas ranches that allow hunting on the ranch, except for a half-mile safety zone around the buildings. I photograph in the safety zone. It is only in such protected places that the bucks get old enough and big enough to have the antlers that look so stunning in photographs.

It is because I photograph in protected areas that I don't get a chance to hunt those deer. Do I ever wish I had a chance to shoot some of the bucks I photograph? You bet I do, but then I wouldn't want to photograph them.

You see, years ago, when I was first starting in wildlife photography, I made a personal commitment to myself that I would not harm or kill any creature that I photographed, and that includes rattlesnakes. I felt that if I could establish a trust between me and the creature I was working with, no matter what it was or where it was, so that I could photograph it, I would not violate that trust by harming the creature. I try to communicate that belief to the creatures I work with through my actions and words, and I sincerely believe that in many cases my message gets through, allowing me to be successful.

I support hunting of deer; they are their own worst enemy because, through overpopulation, they destroy their own habitat and themselves. Regulated sport hunting is the best game management tool we have to work with. I have taken over fifty deer with both the gun and the bow. However, I don't hunt much today. If I have a choice of hunting deer or photographing deer, I'll pick up my camera every time.

I'm never angry at seeing those big bucks that I can't hunt; I just thank God for the blessing of being allowed to see them, to study their behavior, and to photograph them.

You say you have never seen a big-racked buck in Georgia. You just haven't been in the right spot at the right time. I've seen hundreds of photographs of really super deer taken in your home state.

I HAVE LIVED in New Jersey all my life, and have hunted in this state for five years. How big was the biggest buck you ever photographed in New Jersey? Where in the state did it take place? And where can I get a picture of that buck?   *J. B., Lodi, New Jersey*

The largest number of points on a deer that I have photographed in New Jersey was ten, although the points were only two to three inches in length. I photographed this deer on what used to be the Worthington Estate, which is now part of the Worthington State Park.

The largest deer I ever saw in New Jersey was on what used to be the Coventry Hunt Club, which I managed as chief gamekeeper for twenty-one years. This land is now part of the Delaware Water Gap National Recreational Area north of Worthington. I had just discovered a tree four to five inches in diameter that had all of the bark rubbed off it, so I knew there had to be a monster buck in the area. As I was driving down the lane, this huge buck, which had twelve points and at least a twenty-two- to twenty-four-inch spread, stepped out of the woods and paused at the edge of the field down in our game sanctuary. Now I knew how he got to be so big: he was smart enough to stay in the area where no hunting was ever allowed. The distance was too great for a good photograph, but I would have taken a record shot just to prove his existence if I had had a camera along.

We sell both colored posters and eight-by-ten-inch black-and-white photographs of deer at my home. You can write directly to my home or contact me via *Deer & Deer Hunting* magazine. Yes, I do have photos available of that ten-point buck.

I'M GOING TO school to become a police officer but I'm not sure it's right for me. What I'd really like to do is become a wildlife photographer/writer like you. Can I make it?   *M. W. H., Platteville, Wisconsin*

I am asked this question hundreds of times a year by young people who would prefer to spend all of their time in the outdoors hunting, fishing, and taking

The silhouette is a classic shot,
whether in black-and-white or color.

photos. I can only advise you to do as I have done: get a regular full-time job and do your writing and photography as a sideline. If your work is good, you will be able to give up your regular job and switch over to what you really want to do. I was not able to make the switch before I was forty because I had a wife and three sons to provide for. Eventually I made it, but it's not easy. I still work seven days a week, ten to twelve hours per day. Although I am the most published wildlife photographer in North America, I cannot make a good living just selling wildlife photos. In addition, I write books, write four monthly magazine columns, lecture, give seminars, and appear on television and radio as a spokesperson for Cortaid; plus I sell scent, posters, and books through my catalog company.

Don't give up on your idea. It will not be easy, but with the Lord's help you can become anything you want to be, if you are willing to work for it.

IRENE VANDERMOLEN

FREE L. L. RUE
CATALOG AVAILABLE

Index

Italicized page numbers refer to photographs.